TELL OUR STORY, I WILL

TELL OUR STORY, I WILL

One Mom's Journey Raising A Kid With Asperger's Syndrome

JEANNE LEE

gatekeeper press

Published by Gatekeeper Press
3971 Hoover Rd. Suite 77
Columbus, OH 43123-2839

Layout Design by: Mr. Merwin D. Loquias

ISBN: 9781619844957

Printed in the United States of America

DEDICATION

This is dedicated to my small but mighty tribe, Marianne, Sam, Richard and Zach. I love you all.

CHAPTERS

WHY?

"I'm writing a book. I've got the page numbers done."

Steven Wright

YODA HAD ASPERGER'S. Most definitely. He had wacky sentence structure, unwavering focus while he trained Jedi for 800 years, and he did tend to go on and on and on and on about "The Force." The world, nay, the galaxy needs that Yoda and not just the Yoda who plays darts, line dances and is into fusion cooking.

I adore the Yoda man. (Yo-da man!) What a glorious, squatty, fierce, mischievous, wise combo platter of ET, a calm Chihuahua (they exist) with just a touch of an Emerald City munchkin thrown in for good measure, son-of-a-gun. I wish he was real and that we could be besties. And for a very short time, my son, Zach, spoke like him. Tell me I didn't want to rush to the costume store and purchase some toddler Jedi robes and green fuzzy ears. I didn't, but the desire was real.

I guess I've always loved the misfits. (I am one.) I've spent a good deal of my life in the theatre world and those are my people.

Everyone involved in the front, back and sides are my absolute favorites. Interesting, kind, collaborative, crazy-pants, passionate eccentrics, all. Even now, when I enter a theatre, I unclench and feel myself take a deep breath and I know I've returned home.

It's probably strange to compare my first born to a fictional Jedi master, but if Yoda was going through a public school system nowadays, I'm sure he would be ostracized, an outsider. No one would understand him. He might utilize all of his free periods in the gym practicing his lightsaber combat skills or spend too much time alone watching YouTube videos on how to defeat Vader. Yet, he would be the key to saving the universe. We never know; do we?

Why write a book? Well, I tried to find books to read about autism when Zach was little. There was a smattering of choices that included dry clinical explanations or pictures of pretty brain scans or agencies to join. A few books had some personal stories, but they tended to be depressing and scared me a bit. I wanted some personal stories that had some hope in them. Maybe I was craving lightness amidst the stress of the unknown.

If I ask Zach about how he feels about being autistic or the word "autism," he grimaces and I'm sure has a pit in his stomach the size of a popular kid's ego. If I'm completely honest (even though I tell him and wholeheartedly believe that it's healthy to accept who he is, blah, blah, blah), I think I understand. Sure, we all have things to work on, but do I want to accept that I'm a middle-aged, plump marshmallow who has social issues herself and is (probably) never going to be a ballerina or a hip-hop dancer? Damn it, I do not. We're all just here, dealing with our challenges, trying to connect with each other, having some fun.

I want Zach to know that (most) people are amazing and worth the time. Over and over again, making assumptions about people who look or act differently is a huge mistake. If you dismiss someone quickly because they are different in some way, they will lose out and so will YOU. This person in front of you is probably, hopefully, someone whose outlook or humor or perspective is worth a listen. We all have stories to share.

This is my story about Zach and me.

BEGIN THE BEGUINE

"It's delightful, it's delicious, it's de-lovely."

Cole Porter

ZACH WAS MY first baby and I remember being in complete awe of him. My earliest memories are hazy flashbacks of sleepless days and nights on the downstairs brown plaid, 70's couch, and my ex-husband dancing with Zach to Neil Young's "Harvest Moon." I also remember that whenever anyone came to visit, my baby closed his eyes and went away. Now, he definitely could have been a sleepy baby because babies can be that way, but it got to be sort of a weird joke that the second someone other than his dad or I were in the room, Zach's eyes closed, and when the visitor left, he was back.

In the early days, I couldn't figure out how to soothe him. I'd run through my mental checklist; "Ok, I've fed you, changed you, swaddled you, walked you, sang to you; I don't know what to do!" We would walk back and forth, back and forth, and often, I bundled him up and went outside because the daylight seemed to stun him into submission and have a calming effect.

I perfected "the toilet paper dance" which involved putting him on the changing table and swirling long strings of toilet paper in each hand, totally confusing the little fellow. Sometimes a shiny light bulb would do the job. Later, I discovered that mirrors or any reflective objects were Zach's friends; he was completely fascinated by his own image. I thought this was all normal and didn't question it too much.

Then, at Zach's 18-month visit, our family doctor asked how many words Zach had said. "Umm…well, he used to say 'uh-oh' and occasionally 'Momma and Dada' and he has one word, 'key' that really means anything he wants, but that's about it." Our doctor sent us to speech therapy immediately. Zach and I trucked to downtown Seattle every week until he was 5 years old when autism (which I didn't know was his diagnosis quite yet) morphed from a neurological affliction to a mental one. (Really?! I still don't get that one; oh, wait, yes I do … money.)

Our speech therapist really helped us. The most important thing she did was get us to the screenings through our school district for preschool. It's very strange to watch your child be put through a battery of tests (fine motor skills—do this puzzle; bigger motor skills – this obstacle course; talking – have a conversation) and wonder if he is passing. Or actually, you sort of hope he's not passing so you can get help, but also hope that he does pass because what does NOT passing mean? When I found out that Zach would have the privilege of going to special education preschool through our school district, I remember pulling my car over to the side of the road and bawling and bawling. Thank you, universe, for making Zach cute and funny and kind and smart, but also, thank you for getting us all some help because I did not know what to do next.

CLUBBIN' AND WHEEZIN'

"I discovered the wife's got asthma. Thank God – I thought she was hissing at me."

Les Dawson

BEFORE ZACH STARTED school, though, he had some physical issues. When he was born, we were told that Zach had a club foot and that we would need to be proactive immediately. So, on day two of his little life, while we were still in the hospital, they started treating him by manipulating his ankle and foot and putting a teeny-tiny baby cast on his whole left leg. I couldn't believe it; the result inspired one part shock, one part amazement, and a little sprinkle of sad, fairy foot dust. Oh, he was also a little jaundiced. After we went home, we had to return for a few days to put Zach under a lamp, and we had a whole other program for the foot. Every few days, we would have to soak the cast off, bring Zach up to the hospital, and hold him still in a big, cold room on a metal table while they reapplied the cast each time. Eventually, I believe around 6 months, we were told that the casting had corrected a few of the turns in his ankle, but Zach would need surgery to lengthen a muscle on the back of his ankle which would release his foot to be able to rest on the ground. If we didn't do the surgery, he would only be able to walk on his tippy-toes on his left side.

Yeah.

We got through that challenge and then we were told that his feet were different sizes and that the only place to get shoes in the whole city (that would sell us two different sizes) was Nordstrom. We didn't really shop at Nordstrom. Nordstrom was for rich people, for people who bought Kate Spade bags at full price and had shoppers who helped them with their fall wardrobes. However, Zach could get any shoes he wanted and they gave us the two different sizes for the same amount of money as one "normal" pair. I heart you Nordstrom.

When Zach was little, he sort of shimmied around everywhere by using his forearms like he was doing army practices, going from trench to trench, dodging enemy fire. Once I had a woman (who I barely knew) tell me that because Zach had a cast and never crawled properly, his brain didn't get the proper "right, left" action it needed. Bullshit. I'm no scientist (obviously), but people really need to butt out. It's kind of heartless to take a parent of a kid with challenges and offer not-asked-for advice which always comes out sounding and feeling as if the parent was some kind of failure. Plus, it's just messed up to pretend like you KNOW when NOBODY knows. I went to a seminar at the University of Washington when Zach was a toddler. The scientists showed brain scan pictures (which were, again, very colorful and pretty) and DNA strands that may or may not show a propensity for autism (meaning a genetic reason for autism), more research, more research, scientific jargon, blah, blah, blah. But none of it seemed definitive. In other words, the experts were floundering too.

Then, from about 3 years old to the present, Zach developed asthma. When he was younger, it was pretty bad. We ended up in the ER a few times in desperation to help him breath better. I remember one time we had to stay overnight in the hospital with Zach so they could watch him. My ex was on one side of the room trying to sleep and I was on the other side. Zach was so hopped up on the bronchodilator albuterol and steroid treatments that he ran from his dad to me to his dad to me for hours; since Zach didn't really talk, he would shout a letter of the alphabet to each of us. "A," run, run, run, "B," run, run, run, "C," run, run, run……hours of hopped-up fun into the wee hours of morning.

Another time, I went to wake Zach up in his bedroom in the morning, and his eyes rolled back. It was the first and only time I called 911. The paramedics were there in minutes and gave him an inhaler treatment and told me to get Zach to the hospital right away. It wasn't until later I realized I was barely dressed and the house was a mess. Nothing mattered in the moment. Breathing….we all need to freakin' breathe.

When he was around 5, his breathing, especially when he was sleeping, was so painfully loud and labored, I could hear him from the other side of the house. We took him to the doctor's office and found out that one of his tonsils was enlarged; so, back to the hospital. It was not too bad of a blip, and his breathing got way better.

During the time we concentrated on his breathing, we were also figuring out this whole autism thing.

WHEEL. OF. FORTUNE!

"I'm really just a normal person."

Vanna White

ZACH'S PRESCHOOL TEACHER, Tara, asked if I had ever heard of the word, "hyperlexia." Ummm…no. She recommended a book "Reading Too Soon" by Susan Martins Miller (Center for Speech & Language; 1st edition; September 1, 1993) which I started reading immediately. It was shocking. Within the first few pages, the author describes how a child with hyperlexia loves letters and is fascinated by "Wheel of Fortune" and I almost lost it. We had JUST created Zach's 3rd birthday party around the theme of "Wheel of Fortune" (because he absolutely loved that show) and his dad had built a substantial, working wheel to use at the party. (It was a huge hit!) How did this woman KNOW?

Well, she knew because she was the parent of a hyperlexic child and had gathered information from other parents and professionals through interviews, questionnaires and other literature and taped presentations. She really broke it down into 3 aspects: precocious spontaneous reading before the age of five (not a taught skill), difficulty with spoken language (language processing issues) and "abnormal" social skills like an inability to sit for circle time or only parallel playing but not true interaction with other kids. She writes near the beginning of her book,

> "On the one hand, you are relieved that, finally, you have a name, a label, to describe your child and give you a place to start. On the other hand, a label means that you have to accept that your child is indeed different. Your life becomes more complicated than you expected. Your hidden hopes that your child will grow out of this difficult phase are painfully buried in the realization that you must attack the problem head on. Even more significant, you fear for your child's future or your own ability to meet your child's special needs."
>
> **(Miller, 1993, page 4)**

I have a notation by this paragraph. It just says, "Wow." This book laid it out in a very straightforward way. She addressed how hard "transitions" were for these kids. We learned that from an early age, if Zach threw a temper tantrum because of a change in schedule or really for a myriad of unspoken reasons, it could last for hours. We learned to tread so lightly. I know that seems wrong and not really the way to deal with temper tantrums, but even though this was our first child, we could both tell that these outbursts were extreme. They didn't make sense most of the time. He couldn't tell us what was wrong and we couldn't seem to help him. So, we walked on eggshells a lot in the early years.

I remember going to Target with Zach one time when I was very pregnant with my second son. I can't recall what caused the tantrum, but at one point, Zach was on the floor screaming and crying about some atrocity. I tried to get him up; I tried to quiet him, to console him, to get him back in the friggin' cart, but nothing worked. So, I picked him up, lashing and swinging all of his appendages and we high-tailed it out of there. I remember thinking, "I hope he doesn't cause a miscarriage." Whenever I see parents with crying, screaming kids, my first thoughts are of that day. We can't help but be annoyed at parents who can't seem to control their kids in public. It's a natural response. However, for me anyway, about 5 seconds after the annoyance, I want to hug the parents and tell them that I know it's SO hard and that it will (hopefully) pass.

Ms. Miller later wrote, "Developing language is the key to unlocking the hyperlexic child," (Miller, 1993, p. 14). Developing language made EVERYTHING better for us and for Zach. He could explain his confusions; we could negotiate and try to understand better. Transitions became easier because we could warn him and get him excited for what was going to happen after the transition. Her book was full of practical ideas that all seemed to pertain to my boy. Writing lists, visual learning styles, picking battles, school issues were all subjects along the way. I wanted to kiss her for giving me strategies, for giving me an inner tube to hold onto and not drown.

After reading the book, talking with Zach's speech therapist and pondering, my ex and I decided that I would fly out alone to Chicago to attend a "Hyperlexia Conference for Parents and Educators." It was a transformative experience for me; these people were describing my son over and over again.

He couldn't have a conversation with me, but at three years old he could read "The Cat in the Hat" to me verbatim. He hadn't just memorized it; he was reading the words on each page, decoding like a Dick Tracy wannabe. When he did start talking, he did the classic "echolalia" thing. Me: "Zach, would you like juice or milk?" Zach: "Juice or milk." Me: "Okay, would you like milk...or juice?" Zach: "Milk...or juice." (Pause) Me: "Come get what you want!"

Then, the next step involved what I called "**Yoda speak.**" The verb or predicate of the sentence would go first, noun, subject at the end.

> **Zach: "Go to the store, we will?"**
> **Me: (modeling), "Yes, we will go to the store."**

He mixed up pronouns; he repeated phrases of words he learned at inappropriate times, he stared intensely at the ending credits of movies, interested, entranced, as if this was the most influential, critical part of any movie; everything they talked about at the Chicago conference seemed to directly describe what we were going through.

I thought Zach was a genius when he would take a phrase or a saying he heard, and try to plug it into everyday life. That's actually a thing, a smart thing, but a thing. I met other parents, teachers, facilitators and they were all talking about my son. Not really, but kind of….

It's weird – those moments when things fall into focus; it's like when you go to the eye doctor and you look through their fancy lenses and everything is fuzzy…. and then click, click, click; suddenly everything is crystal clear. It was liberating to feel like I understood and wasn't alone. Some of it was hard to hear, but mostly, it was an important, good thing. I felt like I wanted that conference to last forever, that we should move to Chicago and hand these smart people our first born. Of course, that's ridiculous, but hearing all those knowledgeable, talented people did help lay the groundwork for the future of us all.

Full of hope, I was.

"TAKE A LOOK; IT'S IN A BOOK"

Q: What did one book say to another?

A: I just wanted to see if we are on the same page.

Old Riddle

WHEN ZACH WAS 18 months, he basically said the word, "key" for everything or he just didn't speak. He may have said "Mama" or "Dada" once or twice, but those words fell away fast. I remember one of the first times I heard him speak. He was in the back of the car in his car seat, facing forward (it was a different time – back off), and I heard a small voice say, "T-O-Y-O-T-A". WHAT?! Toyota? Was this boy channeling the ghost of a Toyota worker; what the heck? Oooohhhh, I looked forward (we were stopped in traffic) and there on the bumper of the truck in front of us, clear as day, was "TOYOTA." Hmmmm….my boy is a genius! Sure, he wasn't talking, but still waters, people. Still waters.

Letters and numbers were amazing to Zach. He'd go around the house, all excited, reciting 1-800 psychic hotline numbers he saw on the television and had memorized. He'd have a face-off with the television screen anytime the credits to a movie sped by. He was hypnotized by them. We had a stand-up easel for a while that I'd write a "word of the day" on. It was a way to communicate.

So, reading books became very important; this was an opportunity to connect. Zach would sit anytime and stare at the letters in the book while I droned on (I imagine he heard the Charlie Brown teacher voice, *wah-wah-wah....wah-wah)*. I remember when we sat down and HE read his first book out loud to me. I can't remember the exact title, but it was a small, heavy-stock, paper book that could fit in the palm of your hand. The main character was "Gina Giraffe" and Zach used his beautiful little voice and read the whole thing to me. Or did he read it? Was it just from memory?

Maybe it was both. He was definitely decoding words early on. By the time he was three, he would read many Dr. Seuss books, verbatim. He adored watching "Pee Wee's Playhouse." They would flash a "word of the day" and anytime you heard that word, you were supposed to scream like a crazy person. I loved our Pee-Wee time.

It's weird that as Zach got older and acquired more language, he did not like to read. He's a very visual learner and participant in life, and I maintain that the good ole computer replaced his love of books. He got so much more stimuli from computer programs, movies and YouTube. Personally, I *love* reading; I believe I read at least 1 book a week, sometimes 2-3 books, and have done so for decades. I maintain that for Zach, watching Youtube channels of young men playing computer games and goofing around, found a way to fill a companion void. He didn't really have a friend to hang out with, so, he hung out with this faction of people. It's a shame too, because Zach would be an awesome friend. He has great energy and enthusiasm and would just love spending time with some pals. It will happen. Not sure when…..

However, back to reading, it is a magical, special experience that neither of my kids really enjoys (as tweens or teens or young men); I've modeled it their whole lives, encouraged it, read to them, but they really aren't impressed. Maybe that will change for them in the future. I hope so.

"WHEN IN DOUBT, WRITE IT OUT"

"He's making a list

And checking it twice;

Gonna find out Who's naughty and nice…"

**Lyrics from "Santa Claus is Coming to Town"
By: John Fredrick Coots and Haven Gillespie**

"WHEN IN DOUBT, write it out" was a phrase that was used at the conference in Chicago on hyperlexia, and it was my battle-cry, my mantra, and my advice to teachers and aides for many years. If something was written out, it was a rule and it was followed (mostly).

When Zach was very young, I would write out a list for the day. We also posted lists on the refrigerator or walls. Here is one of Zach's first posted lists (probably age 4).

Zachary's Rules
1. Be Nice to Sam
2. Eat Your Food
3. Pee and Poop in the Toilet
4. Use Your Quiet Voice

Then, I started adding the time to his lists (9am = Breakfast, 12pm = Grocery Store). The problem that happened over and over again was that if we were late or wanted to switch the order, IT WAS A BIG DEAL. So, the word "flexible" entered our collective vocabularies. Boy, did Zach hate that word; that word meant something was not going to go as planned and it was going to suck for him. When he started first grade in a regular classroom with an aide by his side, I shared the advice of writing things out. "If you tell Zach to sit down, he probably won't do it. It's like he's hearing impaired, sort of…. It's really like he hears every third or fourth word. The best description I've heard is that of an old-fashioned volume dial that goes from zero to 8 and back down to zero and then up again: that's how he hears. HOWEVER, if you write "SIT DOWN," the chances of him sitting are pretty darn good."

I can still picture his first school aide, Mr. Brannon (a sturdy, big burly young man) running after this tiny first grader with a stack of Post-its and a pencil; "Zach, Zach…read this note!" They actually got along well; Mr. Brannon stayed with Zach a whole year and we were lucky to have him.

Lists have been a big part of Zach's life and I'm certain, will continue to be important. I know for me, lists organize and make sense out of the chaos in my life. This goes for Zach too, but I believe they represent more than that for him (although making sense out of chaos is nothing to dismiss). Zach makes lists of everything, his favorite music, videos, characters, places to eat out, and on and on. It soothes him; it makes sense – it's entertainment to a degree. I love lists too, but I don't have the time or energy or inclination, I guess, to list my favorite of anything.

Age 10 (Things for a Perfect Life)
1. TV
2. Digital Camera
3. Laptop
4. Video Camera
5. Cell Phone

Age 12-Places to Eat (x next to ones I've been to)
1. McDonalds -x
2. Wendy's – x
3. Burger King – x
4. KFC
5. A & W
6. Arby's – x
7. Subway – x
8. Quizno's – x
9. Charley's Grilled Subs – x
10. Taco Time
11. Kidd Valley – x
12. UNeedaBurger
13. Main Street Burgers
14. Wing Dome
15. Baskin Robbins – x
16. Chipotle – x
17. Menchies – x
18. Manna Teriyaki – x
19. Cold Stone
20. Moe's
21. Chili's
22. Orange Julius
23. Carl's Jr.

24. Old Country Buffet – x
25. Top Pot – x

<u>Age 19 – Birthday Wish List for Grandma and Mom</u>
Coded for easy use: really want (*), sorta want (~), don't
really want (.)
1. Fire Emblem: Radiant Dawn for Wii (~)
2. Nintendo 3DS with Legend of Zelda: Ocarina of Time
for 3D (~)
3. Bacon Strips shirt from EpicMealTime.com (*)
4. NCAA Football '12 for XBOX (~)
5. Gift Card Options (Hot Topic, Best Buy, Just Sports)
(*)
6. Toy Story 3 for XBOX (~)
7. Kirby: Mass Attack for DS (~)
8. Zack Ryder Broski shirt from wweshop.com (~)
9. Street Fighter IV: Arcade Edition for XBOX (.)
10. Kirby's Return to Dreamland for Wii (*~)

Why would anyone list what they don't want?

An extension of the written word or rule following were the
many, many apology letters Zach had to write during his school
years. Especially in elementary and middle school, he would
have meltdowns. For me, the term, "meltdown" is a vague word
that many people use and I think is different for each child.
In Zach's case, he would get frustrated. He couldn't say what
he felt or thought; he couldn't communicate what he needed
or wanted and consequently, the situation would escalate.
Sometimes he would respond with just words, sometimes by

kicking or throwing things; as he got older, it was worse for him because he was tall and substantial and even though he wouldn't hurt anyone, his actions came across as threatening. Let's just put it clearly – if you were nearby, you suffered his wrath. When a meltdown happened, there was no "talking things out." During one of these events, it was as though he blacked out. He couldn't say how it started, why, what was said, nothing. I learned to wait at least an hour or two before trying to make sense of what happened. Inevitably, Zach needed to apologize and the best way was through a letter. We also drew up agreements (that were often in list form) that Zach would read, sign and date. They usually worked for a while.

Here's an example of an agreement/apology that Zach wrote, dated and signed in 2002, when he was a third grader. He was angry the day before because at gym, the climbing wall was "shut down" and he threw a major fit.

"Dear Mrs. Hill,

I'm sorry for the way I acted today. I know that big kids don't kick doors and don't throw chairs. If I'm sad I'll take a deep breath and say, "I KNOW I CAN DO IT." I can also write down my thoughts or maybe take a nice walk.

I really like P.E. so I will try my best to have good behaver (sp) and be the best 3rd grader. EVER.

ZACH
4/18/02" (age 11)

Sometimes emails are an easier way to communicate than "in the moment." Zach had a major disagreement with one of his teachers when he was still in high school. They argued about friendships extending past his school time. Friends and social time have been the hardest part of his disability as a young man, and he ended up swearing at his teacher and throwing a fit. After talking with me for a while, he wanted to send his teacher an email. This is what he wrote as a 21-year-old:

"I just want you to know that I had my feelings legit hurt when you were talking about my social life. What I heard out of you/what you implied is that I'm forever alone and that I'll never have friends if I don't do anything. I get that I have to learn to make a move or speak up or whatever, but I didn't really like the way you put it. I KNOW I have to do stuff, that friends don't just happen, but it's a struggle that I'm still trying to figure out.

See, what you fail to understand is that everything takes time and it doesn't just come to you in a snap. I didn't wanna leave school the way I did, but I felt like I was given no other choice. I apologize for it, though. Not because it was wrong, but because I shouldn't have sworn. Sometimes, I think of the phrase "Treat others how you want to be treated." I've been told that a couple of times, and nowadays when I think of that phrase and then people tell me off like you did, it makes me feel like lashing out. And no, I didn't choose to get set off.

You also need to know that on my YouTube channel and on my Instagram, I've had a few comments (one on each) that said, "Forever alone." They were strangers, but it still felt SO bad. When we talked today, and you brought up friendships and being alone, you became one of those hurtful people. You might not have meant it, but that's what I heard.

Friendships are hard for me; I don't know how to call or connect with people. Because I feel as though if I call someone and they're in the middle of something I might hurt their feelings, and doing that makes me just rip my heart out. However, I am going to ask Jordan for his phone number this week and maybe this summer we could hang out once or twice. I also hope once I get in a regular band and a regular job, I'll have more opportunities to maybe get more of a social life.

In closing, I wanted you to know how I felt; I thought that was fair. My feelings were hurt, but I'll try to get over it."

Zach
5/12/14
(Age 21)

As he's gotten older, I forget that writing things down is super helpful. It's important. He is a visual learner and will probably need and respond to lists, agreements, letters and emails for the rest of his life. As a young man in his twenties, he's learned to keep a calendar in his iPod and is able to keep track of his life pretty well with that skill.

ALMOND JOY

"Pete and Repeat were in a boat. Pete fell out; who was left?"

Very, Very, Old Joke

SIDE NOTE ABOUT repeating phrases – I always thought that Zach had a fantastic inclination about learning language. He would pick up phrases from movies or television or books or the computer and then try to plug that language into everyday life situations. Hey, it takes some imagination and some hutzpah to give this a go.

Once when he was going to preschool everyday on a bus and coming home on the bus as well, he got incredibly agitated. I kept trying to figure out what the problem could possibly be (I got very adept at becoming a junior sleuth; everything is a mystery to be solved....Scooby-doo!). Finally, after days of this turmoil, he got off the bus, and stomped his way to the back end of the vehicle, the butt of the bus, if you will. He stared at the number on the side, trying to melt it with his brain.

When he got home that day, "The number is bothering you?" I asked. He nodded solemnly. Huh. So, I watched the number each day and it would change! The bus picking him up was different from the one bringing him home, and sometimes, even those buses were different each day. So, I sat Zach down and tried to explain. "Sometimes, the number is 35; sometimes it's not; it changes; sometimes it's 17; sometimes it's not; sometimes it's 49; sometimes it's not….do you understand?" Zach looked up at me very seriously and replied, "Sometimes you feel like a nut; sometimes you don't?"

Yes. You got it, buddy.

I know people hate labels; I understand and have even felt that way. HOWEVER, I actually felt a sense of tremendous relief when it was suggested by Zach's preschool teacher that my son was *hyperlexic* (no one had said the word "autistic" yet). Hyperlexia seemed to fit Zach, with his love of letters and numbers and his ability to decode and read. This thing, this label of hyperlexia made what we were going through seem approachable, defined, and workable. I was around others who were supporting, educating, and loving my child. We could go from here.

It was around this time that two things happened. One, my mother-in-law, Harriett, gave us a book about autism. What?! Zach's dad and I were appalled and a little incensed. What was she thinking? Our boy wasn't autistic. I pictured autistic kids in a corner, rocking, in their own little worlds. Sure, I could stand directly behind Zach and practically scream his name and get no discernible reaction, but when I opened a soda can in the next room, he would come running. I was convinced that there might be something wrong with his hearing, but we took him in for testing and he passed with flying colors. (For small children, a parent takes the child into a sound-proof booth like on an old time game show. Once in the booth, you sit the child on your lap facing out. Then, teddy bears that are strategically placed in corners of the room make noises and your little one reacts or doesn't react.) So, yeah, autistic? I brought this book and concept up to the speech therapist and I'll never forget the look in her eyes. "Jeanne, think of autism as a huge umbrella; hyperlexia is under that umbrella; it's part of an autistic label." WHAT? Oh, geez......I really could NOT believe it.

I learned pretty quickly that autism has a million faces, multiple facets; the spectrum is huge. I really didn't know it back then, so, this was a very, very hard moment of reality. I always felt like Zach was super smart, so, I also felt like we were going to be okay. I just didn't know how we would get there.

BUBBLE BOY

"I get those fleeting, beautiful moments of inner peace and stillness—and then the other 23 hours and 45 minutes of the day, I'm a human trying to make it through in this world."

Ellen DeGeneres

I READ A fair number of books that talked about sensitivity issues on the autism spectrum. For Zach, he did NOT want to go barefoot in the grass which I figured out during the unfortunate "Hey, let's try the new wading pool" fiasco of '96. And, he wasn't too fond of the vacuum cleaner or a flushing toilet. He didn't like stuffed animals *at all*. (He tolerated an Arthur doll because it wasn't furry).

The big thing for us when he was a toddler was (drum roll) food. Zach did not want to touch it or use utensils or I think, feel food in his mouth. This was a problem. If I could distract him or let him "play" and feed him, he would tolerate it. For a few years, his dad and I would run after him like crazy people with a spoonful of something yelling, "Zach, bite!" His dad joked that in the summer when our windows were open, he was sure that when we yelled, "Zach," the neighbors probably finished the command in their houses, "Bite!" We lived in a small cul-de-sac of 4 houses that were pretty close to each other.

Eating is no longer an issue. Actually, most of the sensitivity issues that Zach started out with are no longer an issue. He still doesn't like touching anything weird or getting dirty.

But, hey, neither do I.

EXPERT, SHMEXPERT

WE WERE TALKED into continuing Zach's school journey with a special education teacher for kindergarten because she was a so-called "expert" in autism. She had dealt with other autistic students and would be a big help to us.

Yeah, that didn't happen.

I don't know if she was going through a hard time when we showed up, but she was SO checked out at this point. I remember going to pick up Zach from school one day and I couldn't find him anywhere. Trying not to panic, I went up to this woman and asked where Zach was. "Oh, he's in the coat closet." Ummm, excuse me? "If he feels agitated, he seems to like to go in the coat closet (a tiny spot filled with coats and boots) and shut the door." I went to the closet, scrunched down and opened the doors; there was Zach all huddled up in a corner, in the dark. "Hey, Zach, it's Mom; come on out."

Once I got him out, I marched up to the teacher and said, "I know you're the 'expert,' but Zach never goes into that closet again; that is no longer an option; let's think of another solution." She thought and suggested a corner of the room where we could put a chair and a headset with books on tape. *What took you so long, lady?* For the love of Pete, what was wrong with her? The one lesson (and an important one for life) is that my immediate response was to pull him out of there, but I let all the other voices override my gut. This woman was the expert; "real" kindergarten would be too intense; blah, blah, blah. My instinct was to get him out of there and because I didn't, it was a terrible year.

YOUNG 'EN'S QUOTES

AUGUST 1998 (6 YEARS OLD): (Zach got a Hot Wheels car in a McDonald's Happy Meal.)

Zach: "Is it hot?"

DECEMBER 1998 (7 YEARS OLD): (Zach's speech therapist showed Zach a picture of a boy with a bloody nose.)

Speech Therapist: "This boy has a problem. What should he do?"
Zach: "He should go to the store and buy a new nose!"

February 1999 (7 years old): (We drive by a FRED MEYER – a store in Seattle. The "F" is not lit up.)

Zach: "Mom! Look! It's RED Meyer!!"

February 1999 (7 years old):

Mom: "Zach, why do you like to look in the mirror all the time?"
Zach: "Because it does what I do."

ASPERGER'S SYNDROME
(COMING SOON TO A THEATRE NEAR YOU)

WE DID GET Zach to a regular first grade in the public school system. Before that transition though, we went to the University of Washington to get a "formal" diagnosis. We had heard that Dr. Geraldine Dawson was a nationally recognized practitioner and she would be able to lead Zach through a battery of tests and give us a written diagnosis that should assist us in getting help at the school.

I don't remember a ton from those few days of testing; I do recall watching Zach through a two-way mirror (like we were at a police station watching Olivia and Elliot from "Law and Order/Special Victims Unit" playing good cop, bad cop with a perp). He was asked to solve puzzles, look at books, answer questions. I remember it took so long that Zach (who tried so hard to keep going) ended up lying down on the table, staring at Dr. Dawson, trying to answer and keep up with the tests. Dr. Dawson even got down on the floor to play trains with Zach and bumped into him, saying "Excuse me!" over and over. She kept repeating this action and Zach never really responded. She attempted conversations; she explored many different avenues of testing and at the end, she spoke with us.

"Your paperwork is going to say Zach is AUTISTIC; this will get you the help you need in the school district. You should be able to get an aide for Zach and other extra support items like a quiet room for testing or extra written materials. I believe that Zach has Asperger's Syndrome, but if I put that on all the paperwork, he probably won't get any help. Don't get me wrong; Asperger's is part of the autism spectrum, but it's at the high end of the spectrum. People with Asperger's are smart and incredibly capable; this is a good thing."

The other thing she said that has always stuck with me (out of a myriad of comments). She told me that as each new challenge came up in Zach's life, whatever it was, we would have to deal with each new thing as a separate entity. She further explained, "You might think that telling Zach how to look both ways for traffic on your street means he should be able to do that action anywhere; this is probably not the case. Streets can look really different and you may have to tell him to do basically the same thing over and over again in different scenarios. As each new scenario plays out in life, Zach may need guidance over and over again with what may seem to you like the same thing, but it's not. It's different. If he knows not to raise his voice when he's at a movie theatre, he may not be able to substitute not raising his voice at a play, because it's not exactly the same thing. Each time, skills will have to be re-iterated." Asperger's. Literal world. No substitutions available.

Asperger's Syndrome. It sounds like an intellectual thriller movie title starring Matt Damon. I couldn't really wrap my head around yet another label. Very daunting.

SANTA, BABY

(7 years old, 12-24-1999)

Dear Santa,
Anything would be fine.
I have been very good.
How about a scuba diver mask?
Your friend,
Zach
P.S. I hope you like the cookies and milk.
ZM

(A little bit older, age 8 or 9)
Dear Santa,
This time I'd like a Nintendo GameCube Machine and
Mario Party 4.
Love, Zachary Lee Merner
P.S. Pretty please with a sugarball on top give these to
me.

(Older age, written in cursive writing)
Dear Santa,
What I so want is Mario Party 5, Mario Kart Double
Dash!!!, and Mario Golf: Toadstool Tour.
Zach M.
P.S. I know I always ask for video games, but there is
some that I've always wanted, and need to ask you for it.

CAN YOU HEAR ME NOW?

"Silly is you in a natural state, and serious is something you have to do until you can get silly again."

Mike Myers

DR. DAWSON WAS correct though. Having a formal diagnosis and conversations with the teachers and principal and staff made a huge difference in our elementary school experience. I give major, major props to our principal. Ms. Wells, who was supportive and onboard from the get-go, was an angel. We had a three-quarter time one-on-one aide, support for the rest of the day when the aide was gone, and a staff that seemed to welcome Zach (and I) whole-heartedly. I found out later that at a staff meeting at the beginning of the school year, our principal introduced Zach and his challenges to everyone and encouraged them to make him feel welcome and to help out whenever possible. Those teachers would all say "hi" to Zach in the hallways, smile, and go out of their way to include him. I'm still touched by their compassion.

Zach's first aide was a young man who was just starting out in special education. He really took it to heart that Zach responded visually and that if he wrote things out, Zach would comply. I can see Zach wandering around the room and Mr. Brannon running after him with post-its and a pen, writing frantically. Zach loved getting up at first; there was so much to look at in the room, the walls were so colorful; there were all those other kids. (Zach loved being around everyone very much—as long as they didn't get in his space too much.) It took a while for him to understand that he needed to sit tight.

He also didn't seem able to sit in a small group in the front of the room with the other kids, listening to the teacher. So, his wonderful teacher said he could listen in the back of the room while doing things on the computer. Of course, my immediate thought was, *But, but....he's not participating; he's not with everyone; this isn't working.* THIS teacher, however, knew what she was doing. I timidly (but firmly) brought up that he needed to go to the front with everyone else. She walked back to the computer section with me. Teacher (Christy), "Hey, Zach, what's the name of the biggest penguins?" Zach (not looking away from the computer for a second but answering without a pause), "Emperor penguins..." Christy, "Very good!" Teacher one, Mom zero.

This was a great lesson in indirect communication. Once I realized that I could have a conversation with my own mother in front of Zach about things I needed Zach to understand, well, a lot more things got addressed. Me: "I love when my kids hang their coats up, Mom. It's so neat and nice, and no one trips over stuff (me, me, I trip over everything)." Done. Coats always hung up. HE COULD HEAR ME IF I DIDN'T TALK DIRECTLY TO HIM. Yowza.

We started to have conversations on the computer. I would type a question and Zach would type back to me. It was super exciting and kind of funny. I had read in some book or other that autistic people didn't have a good sense of humor. Humor was too lofty, too complicated for them to grasp the intricacies of language. *Wrong*. Humor is full of patterns and cadences and Zach grasped humor so well, so quickly. We would listen to "joke" tapes in the car and Zach not only memorized all of the jokes, but he was such a fantastic mimic that he could do the dialects, the timing, the cadences of the joke, spot-on. Very quickly, he could do a 10-minute set at family parties. Yay, a socially acceptable skill to foster and win friends and laughter – and tips (kidding). It was pretty cool to see him blossom, though.

THE COUNT MAKES MISTAKES

"As long as the world is turning and spinning, we're
gonna be dizzy and we're gonna make mistakes."

Mel Brooks

I REMEMBER ONE time when Zach was little, perhaps four
or five years old. We were watching Sesame Street, and the
character of the Count, well, he was counting all wrong. "One
bat, three bats, four bats..." This blew Zach's ever-lovin' mind; it
did NOT compute. How was this possible? The world was not
making sense.

I tried to explain that everyone has an off day; everyone makes
mistakes. He kept shaking his little head. I could see the wheels
turning and this concept did not hold any water.

Such rigidity was a sign of things to come. Even as a young
adult, if something is "wrong," it's very hard for him to tolerate.
Whether *he's* making the mistake or it's someone else's blunder,

it's unacceptable. If it's he who makes the transgression, he beats himself up and has a lot of negative things to say ("I'm so stupid.") If someone else happens to make the mistake, well, GAME OVER. He starts by having a complete knee-jerk reaction which can sometimes lead to seeing the culprit as a nemesis. Zach usually has at least one nemesis in his life at any given time (sometimes more) that completely distresses his soul to the core. He cannot tolerate them; he cannot forgive them; he cannot see another side to the situation.

For example, one of the teachers at his school must have done something wrong at some point because she was a complete idiot in Zach's mind. She could do no right. "She said it was nice day today; it wasn't nice; it was 40 degrees!" I countered with, "It was lovely and sunny today." Zach evaded my lame attempt with, "No, it was cold; she is wrong; she is wrong about everything."

Okay. So, somewhere along the line, this poor woman made a mistake – and somewhere on Sesame Street, in his dilapidated castle, the Count is weeping into his silk cape 'cause he did not make the cut either.

FACEBOOK STATUS

MARCH 2014 (21 YEARS OLD)….

Zach was being down on himself about a mistake he made at school.

Zach: (moaning, head in his hands) "How many does this make?"
Me: (giving him my most serious look) "In every lifetime, you get 800 million mistakes. Not 800 million and one. Got it? 800 million. For everyone. That's how it works."

He smiled.

Finally.

OBSESSIONS

"Cure for an obsession: get another one."

Mason Cooley

THERE ARE SO many stories about autistic obsessions. For the younger set, the literature seems to focus on trains. We actually had some *sweet* train stuff with a proper train table when Zach was younger and he didn't really care for it. At all. So there.

He has, however, over the years, definitely fixated on different things. Some parents might argue that all kids have obsessions with TV shows, trucks, hair ribbons, music. Autistic obsessions are different. They consume the child; their focus is so narrow and complete that it gets in the way of life. Now, that being said, the focus is actually pretty amazing and some of the skills are perfected to a point of pure talent.

Zach went through a pretty heavy phase of taking sports cards and drawing them to scale on bigger pieces of paper, coloring them meticulously and then moving to the next card. I appreciated his artistic eye and his choices; he seemed to always pick cards where the players were in movement and was able to have his own style in the drawings. After he filled two binders with his drawings, I tried to change the groove in the record; I bought him canvases and various sharpies and told him to pick a new subject. He chose Nintendo and video characters and proceeded to draw these very likeable, sweet characters on different sizes of canvas and hang them all over his room. They're very charming.

His wrestling obsession was *not* as charming. I'm not sure how he got interested in WWE, but he truly was consumed for a while. He would imitate vocal patterns, gaits of characters, moves made by different people. We had to ban it for a while. His dad and I would ban various things when he was younger and the result was always heartache and pain. I felt sometimes like the hurt he felt was so deep. Later, he would admit that maybe, *maybe* it was a good thing to take a break, but I'm not sure if he meant it or not.

I don't think "obsessions" are always bad; I think sometimes they open windows for other opportunities. For instance, when Zach was very young, he did not understand or like Halloween. I remember his first Halloween in preschool; his class was going to join in a parade with the rest of the school. I found some black long johns, a Cat-in-the-Hat hat and made a big red bow to hang around Zach's neck. Voila! Cat-in-the-hat costume extraordinaire. He was adorable. However, when he got a glimpse of all the costumes and weirdness of the day, he absolutely refused to put on the hat and bow; he acquiesced to march through all the rooms, but I think it blew his ever-lovin' mind. I heard a meanie mom whisper to her friend regarding

Zach in his black long johns, "What is he supposed to be? A shadow?" You're a hoot, lady.

Pretty soon after the shadow incident, I found a computer program called "Elroy's Costume Closet." In this program, Elroy and a friend got dressed up in different costumes, became different characters, and were in different backgrounds. Zach loved it! After playing with that CD for a while, Zach became very interested in costumes. We would go to a store near our house called "Costume and Display" and visit the hat section. Zach loved different hats. He really had no problem whatsoever with Halloween after a while; I even think we had to "ban" "Elroy's Costume and Display" for a bit because he would *not* stop playing it, thinking about it, printing pictures from it, staring at the pictures – you get the idea.

Little breaks seemed to work. Honestly, it's a good strategy for anyone in life. We all need little breaks; maybe we don't have fixations in the same way, but we all get stuck in life patterns that keep us from really enjoying the world. Facebook, anyone?

JENNY MCCARTHYISM

"So basically, I don't know what I'm talking about. But maybe I do."

Jenny McCarthy

NOT IMPRESSED.

Actually, Jenny McCarthy mortifies me because…

A. She really thought she was saying/doing the right things;
B. SO, SO MANY people listened to her;
C. She had the audacity to try to deny her words and not own up to her mistakes (does she not get that she's left a trail in print and video??).

In the beginning, I'll admit that for about 2 seconds, I was amazed. She what? Jenny McCarthy cured her son of autism? That is beautiful, colossal. And then I took two giant steps back. Ummm, experts and scientists and practitioners and teachers all over the world have never come to the conclusion that autism is curable. Hold the phone.

She's delusional or at the very least, incredibly misguided.

Why is an energetic, beautiful blonde celebrity allowed this much pull and power?

Oh, wait, I think I just answered my own question.

Occasionally I will pick up a magazine at a doctor's office or hair salon and find articles that give me spasms. Why the flying refrigerator would anyone give a crap what Justin Bieber, Ann Hathaway or any person under 40 thinks? Seriously, if you're a young celebrity who has handlers, people, chefs, trainers and managers, I do not under any circumstances care what you are thinking. You live in a beautiful bubble. Enjoy. Deal with whatever your conflicts are and keep your opinions to yourself because the second you start taking yourself too seriously, we have a problem. We get "Jenny-isms." Your truths are your truths – but they most certainly aren't anyone else's truths. This probably goes for anyone under 40, but celebrities wield a mighty sword in today's culture.

So, maybe Jenny isn't entirely to blame for being an asshat. We have to take some responsibility as well.

And the whole "vaccines cause autism thing," well, I'm conflicted. I think – no, I know – vaccines have saved millions of lives. That being said, I have friends who have not vaccinated their kids for different reasons (not autism-related) and while I vehemently respect their decisions, it terrifies me. So, yeah, their kids are fine. I do leave room in my head and heart for the idea that maybe, maybe vaccines can compromise a little one's body. No, no!! Just say no to diseases that have wiped out whole communities. Ahhhhh…. I don't know.

I know from what I've read about vaccines causing autism that there is no conclusive information (or is there??) I've read that the changes most parents see in their children happen at the exact same time as when most little ones get the dreaded MMR. I've read that it's safer, better to get the vaccines, but separate them out and do them one at a time. I don't know. I'm getting to an age where I question everything I read. How am I supposed to take anything at face value? Everyone has an agenda; statistics and reports can be and are skewed.

If I had to do it all over again, I would vaccinate my boy. I'd probably ask them to separate out the vaccines and not give him 10 shots in one day. I'd want to protect him and quite frankly, protect my community as well. I don't believe that vaccines caused Zach's autism. I believe it's genetic. (There are a few people on my side of the family and my ex's family that I believe could have been undiagnosed autistics.) I don't think *not* getting vaccinated would have helped one lick.

And, because I'm not a blonde busty celebrity, no one really cares what I think.

My "Jeanne-isms" are mine alone.

Oh, and by-the-by, wearing dark, horn-rimmed glasses on The View does not make you smarter or make people will take you more seriously, Ms. McCarthy.

Oh, damn it! It probably does.

Sidebar: Pretty quickly after I wrote this short chapter, Ms. McCarthy got booted off "The View" for reasons unknown. I am going to pretend it was because I thought it. 'Cause I did. I wish her well and out of the public eye.

ELEMENTARY, MY DEAR WATSON

"To a great mind, nothing is little."

Sherlock Holmes

ZACH HAD A number of kind souls swirling around him in elementary school. Again, our principal was a treasure, a glittering diamond. For the first year, I kept getting called in to intervene during "situations" (above the few times a week I was going to volunteer there as well). The calls would go something like this: "Hi, Jeanne, this is the speech therapist and well, Zach has positioned himself in the corner of the room and he won't come out or sit down with me or move, really. Could you possibly come over and see what you could do?" (We only lived about 10 minutes away, 5 minutes if I drag-raced over there.)

Once, an earthquake occurred. I'd never been through an earthquake before; in the Midwest where I grew up, Mother Nature threw tornado tantrums. But here in Washington, feeling the earth move under my feet was so weird. As soon as it stopped, the phone rang. I didn't even really hear what they said; I remember just yelling, "I'll be right over!"

I found Zach underneath a table in his classroom. Everyone else was going about their business and the teacher shrugged and said, "He really won't come out." I scrunched down and stared at Zach. He declared, "The earth MOVED." Me: "I know; it did." Zach: "It's not supposed to." Me: "I know. But, I think it's done for a while." Zach: (still shaken) "Okay."

After being called in to the school over and over again, I started to get really worried that this wasn't working and they weren't going to let Zach figure out school. I got a message that the principal wanted to see me. Oh, no! I'm being sent to the principal's office; this cannot be good. I was close to tears and shaking. This very, very compassionate woman looked at me and said, "I just wanted to have a moment with you, Jeanne. I want you to know something. Everyone in this school wants Zach to succeed; all the teachers know who Zach is and what he needs and no matter how long it takes, I want you to know that this is Zach's school. He belongs here; this is his home." I don't know how we got so lucky. To this day, I am thankful and grateful to the principal and to every person at that school. Her attitude really did trickle down to every teacher in the building. Certain teachers went out of their way to cultivate friendships with Zach.

There was a wonderful woman, Georgia, who did a variety of jobs at the school (helped in the kindergarten rooms, recess, lunch and on and on); she looked out for him the whole time he was there; we're talking 6 years. She was a consistent teacher/

friend that he (and I) could count on. "Hey, Zackers...come with me," she would say to him and they would traipse off together and take a walk, or go run an errand. She helped him when he was having a bad day and made it a good day. I love her forever. She extended herself to many, many children and their parents...knitting hats for a little girl who pulled at her hair, making sure certain kids ate their lunch or even *had* a lunch, and on and on. The world is full of special people who do go out of their way to be kind. My heart gets so full when I think about these incredibly lovely folks.

I AM NOT AN ANT!

"But I don't wanna be a Pirate!"

Jerry Seinfeld

ZACH (3RD GRADE HOMEWORK)

Me: So, your teacher wants you to write a story.

Zach: Okay.

Me: You need to pretend you are an ant at a picnic. Write about it.

Zach: I'm an ant? I'm not an ant.

Me: Oh, I know! This is just a pretend…. just PRETEND you're an ant at a picnic. Just describe what you see.

Zach: BUT I AM NOT AN ANT!!

Me: Can't you just close your eyes and try to picture it?

Zach: No. I'm not an ant.

Me: (Pause) Okay; you're Zach and you're at a picnic. Write about it.

Zach: Can we go on a picnic?

Me: Sure. Soon. Can you write your story?

Zach: Okay.

FLEXIBILITY

"All generalizations are false, including this one."

Mark Twain

During Zach's early years, there were a number of "cures" that were presented to us. I believe during his kindergarten year, there was a special computer program being touted as the best thing for autistic children. The children would do these programs for hours each day and come out the other end of the tunnel. I initially got super excited; what is this magic? How can it help my boy? Our speech therapist at the school said she would go to the information session and report back to us. She came back with a resounding "NO." She stated that she had never been in a room with a harder sell than these carny people and that included some very aggressive car salesmen she had dealt with in her life. She acquiesced that maybe, maybe it might have some good points, but, honestly, the people running it would not have to push so hard if it worked. If it was truly effective and so promising, it would sell itself.

I never heard of this program ever again.

Then, there was the national news item that a mother had taken
her son in for digestive issues and the medicine that the boy was
given cured his autism. There was a mad run for this medicine
all over the country and nothing conclusive was ever brought
up again.

Or how about the lady in the check-out lane at our grocery
store who thrust her business card in my hand? She was a
proponent of something called "crawling therapy." If your son
went straight to walking, having crawling therapy will realign
his right and left brain hemispheres and help him for the rest of
his life.

Please.

I got so tired of people trying to prey on me and others who
were desperate for answers. We tried a lactose-free diet for a
while and also a gluten-free diet (before it was fashionable and
there were products everywhere). It was super hard; we didn't
do it for very long, and I got very discouraged. Changing a diet
seemed to make some sense to me, but again, I was afloat in a
vast ocean of loneliness and con artists.

My conclusion pretty early on was this: There was no cure.
My job was to figure out how to help Zach with coping skills.
He was incredibly smart. I would watch him; he constantly
observed everything around him and tried to figure things
out. I could help him deduce; I could help him with strategies.
Sometimes it was difficult to find the right words. We went
through a "this is one of those times when you have to be
flexible" stage, a phrase which would cause him to moan and

groan. Flexible meant he couldn't have things his way. Flexible was bad. "Let's be more pliable." What?! *Ummm, let's go with the flow; let's try to be more easy-going.* Yeah, he was smart. He knew what I was doing and he didn't like it one bit. This did NOT make him autistic; this made him a kid.

I actually struggle to this day with that concept, more so when he was younger. "Is this an autistic thing or a teenager/human being thing"? More often than not, it was a kid thing. Parents everywhere are wringing their hands and getting gray hairs over the decisions their young 'ens are choosing – or not choosing. This angst is universal and even more so for Ms. I-Can-Control-Everything-In-My-World-I-Really-Can—Amen.

COMPUTER CONVERSATIONS

"I've failed over and over and over again in my life and that is why I succeed."

Michael Jordan

EVERY ONCE IN a while, when I wanted to talk to Zach and it seemed too hard, or sometimes just for the heck of it, we would sit at the computer and type a conversation with each other. No talking was allowed; I would type something and he would type back. Here's an example from March 2001 (age 12). At the time, we were having major issues with winning and losing at home and at school – temper tantrums and such.

Mom: I would like to talk about winning and losing.
Zach: Well……alright.
Mom: What do you think about winning?
Zach: Great!
Mom: Do you like to win?
Zach: Always.
Mom: Do you think that you should win all the time?
Zach: I think so.

Mom: What about the other people in the world—should they always lose?

Zach: I don't know……maybe here in Washington.

Mom: Should everyone in Washington lose?

Zach: No way.

Mom: BUT—if *you* always win, someone has to always lose. Is that fair?

Zach: Maybe.

Mom: Okay, Zach. Would *you* like to always lose?

Zach: No way.

Mom: Why not?

Zach: I don't like losing.

Mom: Nobody likes it.

Zach: Yeah, I guess you're right.

Mom: Soooo…maybe the fair thing, the RIGHT thing is that sometimes you get to win and sometimes you have to lose.

Zach: I'd be smarter if I were you.

Mom: What's so smart?

Zach: Um……I don't know.

Mom: Okay, Zach…do you know that you have to be a nice loser and learn from your mistakes?

Zach: Of course I do.

Mom: What does it mean to be a GOOD SPORT?

Zach: Say congratulations.

Mom: Great!! Can you be a GOOD SPORT?

Zach: I hope so!

Mom: I KNOW you can do it. Great job.

Zach: I love you always.

Mom: Ditto ditto spitto. 4-ever!

(He has gotten better at the whole winning and losing concept, but even as a young adult it's hard. He takes it to an extreme sometimes. For example, he was pretty shook up when the Miami Heat did *not* pull off a "three-peat" win for the basketball championship in 2014. He was mad at the whole team, mad that it didn't happen, and mad that he was helpless to change the outcome. However, he pulled it together within a day or two. As a younger boy, losses such as this could linger for weeks. I remember vowing to never watch American Idol with him – because he was devastated when his picks didn't win. I think my breaking point was the year Carrie "UnderPants" won. He really despised her at the time. He seems to live vicariously through the wins and losses, as if he himself is winning and losing. The average sports fan is of this ilk too; it's just that Zach takes it to the extreme.

A ZACH APOLOGY FROM SCHOOL
(OCT. 2004, 11 YEARS OLD)

"I flung a post-it for the 4th time and I'm so, so, so, so, so, so, so, so, so, so, so, so, so, so, so, so, so, so, so, so, so, so, so, so, so, so, so, so, so, so, so, so, so, so sorry."

(Are you sure, honey? Are you really, really, really, really sure??)

ONE-ON-ONE, OVER AND OVER AGAIN

"When I was a boy and I would see scary things in the news, my mother would say to me, 'Look for the helpers. You will always find people who are helping.' "

Fred Rogers

EVERY YEAR I thought it was my job to write up something for the new aide. As I have mentioned before, Zach ended up having a three-quarter time aide for most of his elementary and middle school years The aides usually lasted the entire year because on the whole Zach was an easy one-on-one.

I remember one year, his new aide came to the first meeting wearing steel-toed boots. "Why?" I asked (pointing at her footwear).

"Well, my last kid stepped on my feet all the time; he broke my toe."

Wow. "Well, you're safe with Zach; he'll either ignore you or hug you."

Some of his aides "got it" and some didn't. I sincerely didn't mind if they didn't get him as long as they tried and were kind. That didn't always happen, but on the whole, we had a ton of success with our aides. Many of them wanted to go into special education or had training with autistic kids; some of them were parents in the district, and a few of them didn't care or were just Negative-Nellys. I'm not sure why <u>they</u> were there, but it happens.

Every year, I would try to write a one page helpful hint page; I figured I could probably hold someone's attention for at least a page. The page usually consisted of a list telling them things like Zach's current interests, current phrases that seemed to mean something, things we were working on, and a reminder that he was a visual learner. For years I tried to include that special phrase, "When in doubt, write it out." This really worked through many grades. It still works. If something is written down, Zach understands it immediately and really treats whatever it is with more reverence. Anything written down must be true, the right thing, and the law.

One aide in high school stayed with him for 3 years. Natasha. Natasha was very shy and did not speak English well. I was SO against her – at first. "How can you give a kid who struggles with language someone who can't speak English well? How is this ever going to work? I don't understand; please find someone else, please." The team at the high school pretty much just shook their heads; there wasn't anyone else (according to them), and I actually believed them. We met with her many times over the years, and she couldn't have been more stellar. She tried *so* hard and put in such effort. She cared that Zach was progressing; she looked up things for him; she talked with him, complimented him, confronted him; she was amazing, really.

I, of course, think my son is lovely beyond compare, but I'm sure that he was not always kind to her. I'm positive he gave her a ton of attitude. I always made sure that Zach knew that Natasha was to be treated with respect and kindness and that no matter what, she was looking out for him, that she was a blessing. She communicated through a spiral notebook that went back and forth (pre-emailing) and she seemed to gather more and more understanding and confidence as time went by. She even came to the high school graduation ceremony and brought *me* flowers. How could I have been so far off in my evaluation of someone?

Every year in elementary school, middle school and even in high school, his aide time came up. Quick sidebar regarding IEP meetings (Individual Education Plans): These once-a-year (or more) meetings between we, the parents, and the school members involved concerning Zach's educational progress were on one hand, emotional (I always pictured the Grinch when his heart grew three sizes in one day) because we would be sitting around a meeting table full of teachers and administrators in a tiny room, and their whole focus was on our kid. Seriously. I almost wept a few times. They also commented on past goals and future goals and in that respect they were completely and utterly brilliant.

However, the dark side of this moon was that they were constantly trying to cut his aide time. I sort of understood. Funding for public schools is ridiculous and especially for special education. Zach really needed his aide time though. All that verbal stuff was overwhelming for a kid who learned visually. The threats and ultimatums and "Let's Make a Deal" comments came every single time.

Here's the thing; I don't like threats. I don't respond to platitudes either. Also, I can be sort of "doormat-y" for myself, but *not* for my kid. I need an explanation or at least a dialogue. My response to the "real world" comments was simply, "I don't think school is much like the real world; however, his diagnosis does suggest that for Zach to succeed in the school world he does need support and we've seen that having an aide has helped him to be successful."

I even had a bus mom "friend" ask "Umm…why does Zach get an aide? All kids would be more successful with a helper." Really? Geez, this lady had spent time with Zach over a few years; needless to say, we did not hang out after that point. I was very disappointed in her. Being special needs is not always crystal clear to an outside viewing (and even, I guess, with family and friends because they don't always see the whole picture). I wanted to scream at her; I wanted to say "YOUR KID DOESN'T HAVE AUTISM; YOUR KID KNOWS HOW TO JOIN GROUPS AND HAVE CLOSE FRIENDS; YOUR KID DOESN'T HAVE PROBLEMS HEARING ALL VERBAL CUES." I think I just shook my head and said, "Agree to disagree…." And then never called her again. Passive-aggressive *is* my middle name. Or maybe I'm just a non-confrontational girl and idiot remarks are my Kryptonite.

I never wanted Zach's aides to follow him around like a shadow; I always hoped they were there for the whole classroom (and for Zach in times of distress or confusion), but mostly for the whole room. That way, everyone would benefit. I was made to believe that this was the case most of the time.

We did have some glitches along the way. There was one lady who really liked and connected with Zach (which is major, not discounting that positive). But she really couldn't help him much in the classroom or connecting with others. Zach found a lot of coins that year. They would actually go around looking in the hallways and the parking lot for change on the ground; Zach found a ton of ground swell. But, why wasn't he in class? What the hell? He really liked this woman though, and she seemed to understand his motivations as well; they would have made great buddies. She actually called about once a year and invited Zach out for lunch; how sweet is that? But she really didn't help him too much at actual school. It was possible that at that point, perhaps that was all he was capable of achieving, but my hopes were a bit higher. It's hard to be upset at someone who shows so much kindness and concern for your kid.

For most of elementary, middle and high school, we sent a notebook back-and-forth with Zach. The aide would jot his homework down, and include any highlights or challenges. In turn, John and I would work with Zach on any issues and write back about the night or anything noteworthy to the aides. It was a pretty good system. Nowadays, I'm sure we would email. I found some of the notebooks recently and they brought up so much. One was from his fifth grade year. Some of the highlights include *not* wanting to see his friends in a musical at school (he loves music, but doesn't want any part of hearing the singing in a play), some "meltdowns," and how much he loved being a lunchroom helper.

Many of his school pals were in a production of "Sleepy Hollow" (the musical!), and Zach was beside himself. He wanted no part of witnessing it. Honestly, unless it's your kid or you're somehow invested in some other way, I'm not sure many people would WANT to see a fifth grade musical version of "Sleepy Hollow." I had a hard time even typing that last sentence.

(2004)

Zach: "I don't want to see SLEEPY HOLLOW!"
Me: "It's OK. I checked the book out of the library. You'll know the whole story. You won't be scared."
Zach: "I'm NOT scared. I just don't want to see my friends—singing."
Me: "If your friends were in a play, just talking, would that be OK?"
Zach: "Yes."
Me: "Zach, I don't understand. Your friends are singing. What's wrong with that?"
Zach: "I can't explain it. I just hate it." (Starts to cry)
Me: "Are they not singing in tune? Is it because they're up on stage? What is it?"
Zach: (cannot verbalize an answer)
Me: "Ok, Zach. I don't get it, but that's OK. Honestly, I can't guarantee anything, but I'll ask if you can just stay at school and do homework or help a teacher out. You might have to go to the play, but I'll ask, OK?"

Zach: "Thanks, Mom! You're the best."
Me: "Zach, I don't know if I can make them understand, but I'll try."
Zach: "Okay."

In the end, Zach did not go. He stayed at school. He communicated to his aide later that he was also upset to NOT go too, but not because of missing the play; he was scared his friends would be mad at him. Pretty elevated thinking, I'd say.

I guess in the end, I'm so glad we lived in a school district that really tried to support Zach. I'm grateful we got the initial diagnosis that helped support his needs; it really opened the first windows. I'm thankful for all the aides, teachers, staff members, bus drivers, bus moms and everyone we met who seemed to care. Caring is highly underrated and it changed our lives, really truly.

COMEDY TONIGHT

"Is a hippopotamus a hippopotamus, or just a really cool Opotamus?"

Mitch Hedberg

I'M NOT SURE it was a super conscious decision, but I ended up having a handful of joke tapes and CDs for the car that I put on all the time when the kids were young. Jim Gaffigan was pretty clean; Garrison Keillor had some "third grader jokes" that were fun, and we wore out a very weird cassette tape with Carol Channing and a group of children's voices called "Kidding Around." Well, Zach not only learned all of these jokes verbatim, but mimicked the dialects, inflections and timing perfectly. It was my first real inkling of his capacity for memory and imitation. As time went on, he could imitate voices and the physical tics and movements of characters as well. He would then, with very little prodding, perform his jokes at family parties. The boy had a strong 10-minute set that killed. Honestly, it was so nice for him to be able to feel comfortable socially doing something that everyone liked.

Some of his later interests were harder to understand. He would talk about video games, characters, onscreen scenarios ad nauseam (like a lot of kids), but it was a little more frenetic than most kids, more purposeful and he would repeat stuff often. I would get confused and have to ask him to explain what something he was spouting came from. After a while, I think it really frustrated him, but I thought it was fair for him to realize that not everyone was seeing and hearing what he was; we were not all on his page.

I read somewhere in my early readings that people with autism did not get humor. I get it. Zach was very literal. I showed him books with phrases like "Raining Cats and Dogs" and I remember his eyes getting huge. When he was little and someone would laugh, he'd whisper in my ear, "Was that a joke?" As he got older, if someone laughed, he would sometimes interpret the laughter as a sign of disrespect and he would lash out. It was hard for him to get the joke when he really didn't get the joke. That being said, Zach is himself hysterical. He often cracks me up with his impressions and word play. Yes, sometimes it's repetitive, but he totally gets the humor now.

When he was around 5 years old, we had a little routine at bed where I would say good-night, turn off the light, shut the door and then after a few seconds, I would open the door and whisper, "Are you asleep?" Zach would then snore obnoxiously. We did this exchange for months. Cut to Zach in his twenties; I happened to say good-night one evening and I turned off his lights. I then heard, "Hey, ask me if I'm asleep." What? I didn't get it and quite frankly was slightly annoyed. "Zach, what are you talking about?" "Ask me if I'm asleep!" So, I asked him in a frustrated tone, "Are you asleep?" (Pause) SNORE, SNORE, SNORE....I shut his door and THEN I GOT IT. I couldn't believe it! He was remembering our routine from 15 years ago. I opened the door and whispered it one more time. "Are you asleep?!" SNORE, SNORE, SNORE....

Amazing. He has a jaw-dropping memory and a king-size sense of humor.

TV-LAND

WHEN YOU TAKE your child in for their "well-visits," the doctors and nurses always reiterate that it's best to limit TV. Which makes sense. TV is horribly addictive and really about commercials, and some of the images are not what you want to plant in your dear, spotless, new baby's brain. However, the advice we got with Zach was to watch as much as we wanted because the more TV, movies, and computer programs we engaged in, the more he was going to acquire language.

All of this watching predated YouTube, Google, and high-speed Internet; I had dial-up for far too long and went even longer before getting Wi-Fi; at age 53, I still don't have a smart phone. All this technology freaks me out on so many different levels. When I walk into the lunch room at work for my half hour lunch, everyone's head is down, looking at their phones. I think it's sad. It makes me feel lonely and out-of-touch.

However, we did watch (probably) too much TV. The shows engaged Zach. He and I could sit next to each other and watch Pee Wee's Playhouse and scream together when Pee Wee said the word of the day and laugh together at his silliness (thank you, Paul Reubens).

When "Blue's Clues" came on the scene, I scoffed. What a bizarre show! A 2-dimensional, rudimentarily drawn dog and a human young man – finding clues to solve simple problems…..I was wrong. That show opened Zach up to his first drawings. He would draw the clues and then he started drawing everything. Zach is a fantastic artist. I remember one summer giving him some sidewalk chalk and he drew every clue he could muster; most of the cul-de-sac was covered in his drawings. His dad went up to our roof and took a picture of all these drawings with Zach sitting on the ground, looking up, surrounded by the images. It looked like Zach's brain had exploded on the asphalt.

Another favorite show that a friend recommended was "Mr. Bean. Mr. Bean did not help with language, but we had so much fun laughing at Rowan Atkinson. It's mostly physical comedy and Mr. Atkinson is a master artist. Mr. Bean was such a fun, lovable, dorky guy and his stories and humor were engaging (now there are cartoons of Mr. Bean; they're fantastic!).

We watched everything, including Sesame Street, Mr. Rogers, everything on Nickelodeon and some Disney things. These shows did help. They helped with language and helped us connect to something together. In later years, there were things that were NOT helpful. Zach has spent too much time on the computer looking at wrestling, video games, music stuff—much of it has been inappropriate (in my estimation) and because his did and I worked full time, he spent too much time on these items. These games definitely became a babysitter, an obsession, an easy out. However, because Zach didn't have friendships, some of these YouTube sites became surrogate friends. He really enjoyed these personalities and identified with their interests. They were his age and he could feel like part of a group. It was hard for me to discourage it because it made up for a part that wasn't there – he belonged.

Hopefully, Zach will develop some friendships at work or in music; hopefully the addictive part of his computer life will dissipate easily. We ALL watch too much TV, Google too much, Facebook too often. These activities start to take the place of real, meaningful human contact. How can we nurture our family and friends when we have to catch up on the Daily Show and peek in on all of our Facebook friends and create that Instagram or Vine? I would much rather call a friend on the phone than find more Pinterest pictures, but I will admit that for me – at least right now – Facebook is a complete time-suck and I couldn't be more ashamed that I've reached level 160 on Candy Crush. It represents so much "going away" time; it makes me feel like the hermit I always joke that I am.

OPPOSITE DAY

SpongeBob: "I love…I mean, I hate Opposite Day. (Giggles as he runs back into his pineapple) I'm not ready!"

Season One – SpongeBob – "Opposite Day"

I HAVE HEARD the phrase "having your son in my class isn't fair to the rest of the class". Asshat. Really? Okay, it was one person, but c'mon. Seriously, this is such a douche-y declaration because in my experience, in my reality, it is the opposite. Opposite day! Especially in elementary school, I saw kids reach out, nurture, laugh, explain, lead, discuss, and all around enjoy the experience of having Zach in their classes. My ex-husband and I tried to be present during that time; he built an amazing stage out of an old futon frame and we put on elaborate puppet shows for the school, went on field trips, made our presence known. These children did NOT see Zach (or us) as different; well, maybe they did, a little, but they didn't seem to care. Zach had energy, personality, and kindness emanating from his pores. (He's always been a very likeable chap.) He played piano and told jokes at the 5th grade talent show (huge success), went on the overnight 6th grade camping trip, and went to birthday parties in our neighborhood. Being different should not EVER be a reason for exclusion; I know it is sometimes, but aren't people who look different, act different, the most special-est among us? I adore people who see the world differently; they make the days more interesting and richer and way, way more fun.

I often feel TOO normal. How did a shy Midwestern gal who loved to pretend and become different characters and tell stories become a middle-aged, chubby divorcee raising two kids and still struggle to find a bit of fun? I'm a stereotype living inside a cliché.

BORING….give me different any day.

SO, THIS HAPPENED

I REMEMBER THE call. Zach had just started 1st grade and the phone rang. The principal stated, "Jeanne, Zach just hit another boy on the head with a rock." What, the – what?! "Don't be too upset, the boy is fine; Zach is fine; it happened at recess today." I couldn't believe it. What happened? Did it matter what happened? My boy hit another boy with a rock? "Do the parents want to meet with me? The teachers?" The principal hesitated, "Well, I spoke with the boy's mom, and, and she's fine…. she said, 'He probably deserved it.'"

Chill mom with a sense of humor for the win…..

AND THEN, THIS HAPPENED

So, NO MORE violent acts took place until middle school. I remember this call as well. "Jeanne, Zach has been suspended for 3 days because of a hitting incident."

Here's how it went down. Zach was getting a juice from a vending machine at lunch and some kid came right up to him and said, "You're a retard, right? Are you a retard?" No one (to my knowledge) had ever badmouthed Zach or used this word towards him. It was reported that at this point, Zach just stared at the kid in disbelief, sort of frozen in time. Punk kid says, "I bet you want to hit me; go ahead; hit me; HIT ME!" So, Zach did. He walloped him good (from what I hear), one punch to the gut. Both kids got pulled into the principal's office; both kids got suspended. How do I know what happened? This punk man-child reported how it happened. Let's call him Hulk Hogan; Hulk said, "I shouldn't have done it; it was all my fault; I never thought he'd actually hit me; I take all the blame."

Bully for the bully because Zach couldn't have, at that point, told me what happened. I'm not sure why this little heathen fessed up, but he did. Hulk was never heard of again.

SURPRISE!

"Reality continues to ruin my life."

Bill Watterson

For a long, long time, Zach could not tolerate or be in the same room with babies, small children or cats and dogs. They were all too unpredictable, too unstable. Where were they going? They would bark or cry or jump or slobber on you.

When Sam was born, Zach was about 3; we were in the midst of all this new information, figuring stuff out, preschool, speech therapy; it was very hectic. I remember asking Zach to draw some pictures for a timeline for a first grade project.

The year Sam was born, Zach drew two people facing each other in profile (one little person, one bigger guy); the little one was smiling sweetly and the bigger figure (Zach) had tiny, pinpoint eyes and a mouth shaped in a big open "O." It was a look of complete surprise, dare I say, shock. I'm sure those were his true-blue feelings, utter disbelief.

Zach has grown so much; he quickly relaxed his view on babies and small children.

Cats and dogs can still suck it though.

I remember when he was about 5 years old, our neighbor, Trudy, brought over a tiny, 3 week old, soft, beautiful, TINY kitten. It fit in the palm of her hand. Well, Zach took one look at that thing, screamed bloody murder and ran to his room and slammed the door. He then opened his bedroom window screaming for the kitten to go away.

I've never had an animal growing up or as an adult, but it crossed my mind many times to get one to try to get Zach over his immense fear of cats and dogs. I felt that it COULD help or it COULD send him into many years of therapy. Hard to tell.

So many things that made Zach anxious have fallen away; I hope that his fixation on cats and dogs can relax as time marches on. Part of me wonders if worrying about dogs is partly a survival instinct. Who am I to tinker with his protective inclinations? I'm afraid of heights, spiders and the dark, and I wouldn't exactly appreciate someone forcing me to deal with those fears. The dog thing is hard though. If Zach sees a dog while he's walking, he'll cross the street quickly or start running. His dad's neighborhood has a dog that Zach is super vigilant about. He avoids it at all costs, anytime, anywhere. The dog torments him. We've offered to have him talk to a therapist, but honestly, I worry about forcing him to do things he's not ready to do.

His dad asked him once, "If you could spend a day with a friend and play video games that you chose and have snacks and fun, but there was a dog in the house in the next room that would never, ever get near you, would you go?" Zach hung his head and thought for a second and whispered, "I'd have to pass." Poor guy.

MEMORY MAN

"I have a memory like an elephant. I remember every elephant I've ever met."

Herb Caen

ZACH HAS ALWAYS had an incredible memory. I remember when he was about 4 years old, we put an open curio shelf in his room that had about 30 separate openings in it right by his bed. We put all of his special friends in those holes, Blue from Blue's Clues, Garfield, Mario, Luigi, Elmo, Oscar and on and on. Each slot had a little plastic figurine. I don't know why I did it, but a few times I switched 2 of the characters. If Elmo was on a top slot, I moved him to a middle slot. Then, I'd move Mario from the middle slot to the top slot. That's it. Then, I'd watch Zach as we entered his room under the guise of reading a book. In less than a minute, he'd notice something amiss and pluck those 2 wandering toys and put them back in their proper places.

He would and did remember everyone's name. I remember at Christmas or the end of a school year, asking Zach the name of his bus driver, so that I could write a thank you card. Or I'd ask what was the name of that clerk at the grocery store who was so nice? He knew every time.

That's not to say he remembered everything. He remembers things that capture his attention. He took piano lessons for a few years (I believe age 7-10) and he could NOT remember the names of the notes to save his life. We'd go over and over them and he'd get so mad. The thing is he really didn't enjoy playing the piano, but he was great at it. He'd watch his teacher play and within minutes he could replicate her rhythms and hand placement. So, why did he have to learn the notes; he didn't need no stinkin' notes!

As a young adult playing the drums, his teacher, Mike, said that Zach would bring in some complicated drum music that he obviously didn't practice; they would go over it and pretty quickly, Mike could tell that Zach wasn't looking at the music anymore; he was playing perfectly from memory. Mike, who was an accomplished drummer in our fair city, was very impressed by Zach's memory and skill. Zach then joined a band through the Seattle Drum School and I asked him where his music was. "I don't have any." Well, of course, he must have music. "Where is it, Zach?" He tapped his forehead; "Right here." Ohhhhh, okay, got it.

I think that whatever Zach's future holds, his memory will serve him well; as someone who has left her mid-life crisis blowin' in the wind, a brilliant mind is to be cherished.

CAPE FEAR

"When the dog bites, when the bee stings
When I'm feeling sad
I simply remember my favorite things
And then I don't feel so bad."

Rodgers and Hammerstein

I OFTEN FOUND myself in the position of being a junior detective (Jeanne "Nancy Drew" Lee) especially when Zach was younger. Because language was not very present, I would have to rely on my wits to figure out what the issues were, gather clues, and call the Hardy Boys for back-up.

Often, Zach's fears were the cause of his hysterics. For instance, when he was five or six, he didn't want to go into the grocery store. He would actually go into panic mode; he would hold my hand really, really hard and I just didn't get it. I think one time he managed to say the word, "holes." *Holes? There aren't any holes in the grocery store; what does he mean?*

Finally, I crouched down to reassure him and as I gazed over the grocery store floor, I noticed how shiny and reflective it was. It was almost like a body of water on a sunny day, translucent, sort of invisible. Does the shiny floor look like a hole to Zach? Huh. Maybe. "Show me the hole, Zach." He pointed to the floor. "It's not a hole, honey; I tell you what; I'm going to put you in this cart; it will keep you safe; it will not fall in a hole. If you're in the cart, it will keep you safe." After that time, he was much better.

Then there was a time he refused to go into the dining room. For the love of Pete, what was the deal now? Normally, a little person could give you a hint about what was going on, let you know verbally, but Zach couldn't. I finally figured it out. It was around Halloween and I had put a very friendly, smiling, ceramic jack-o-lantern on the dining room table. Zach seemed terrified of that pumpkin; I had already decided that nothing scary would go up, only pumpkins. Yeah, that didn't work. That pumpkin didn't surface again for years.

Other fears included flies ("they will eat me"), dogs, and thunder. The dogs and thunder make sense to me, and honestly, we all have rational and irrational fears. As the years go by, it's much easier to suss out the challenges because Zach has language skills and can mostly tell me what's going on. This doesn't mean I can change his thinking, but I don't think anyone could get me to capture a big spider and set them free in the yard. I know I'm bigger than the spider, but I'm not touching that sucker.

How about the demon dogs in our neighborhood? There were two German Shepherds who would throw themselves against their fence every time we went to get the mail or walked to and from the bus stop. Barking, jumping up and down, pounding against their rickety fence (which broke a number of times) were normal. I, of course, tried to lighten the mood. "Oh, they're just saying 'hello'! Hello, doggies!!" Zach didn't buy it for a second; when he got near the fence, he'd throw his arms up in the air, scream bloody murder and run for the hills. One of the dogs was named "Hans." At some point, Hans escaped and trapped a neighbor in his garage, snarling and barking; the neighbor shot him. No more Hans. It's sad to say, but it was a huge relief for our family. The other dog (Fritz) barked, but was way more chill and never got out.

We all have fears and worries (that are justified), but when you can't communicate well, I think it must be exasperating. You can't ask questions or get out your feelings or figure out how to deal with all the challenges that occur. I still maintain that when I watched Zach walk to the bus stop in first grade with a backpack almost as big as he was, and a huge smile, ready to meet the day, he was the epitome of bravery. I was always so grateful that my boy wanted to be a part of this confusing thing called life. He reveled in people and school and managed to stay incredibly positive.

DIVORCE

"Getting a divorce really sucks."

Amy Poehler

WHEN ZACH WAS about 10, my husband and I decided after 16 years of marriage, that we were not moving on. Well, he decided and after reading a few articles and books, we sat the kids down and said "WE'VE decided this is the best course of action; WE love you always and forever; WE will work this out so that everyone is comfortable, but we are getting a divorce." Etc., etc., etc. I would have bet money that Sam would fall apart and that Zach would take it somewhat in stride, but I would have lost that bet.

Zach let out a wail that I compare to keening women from the Middle East facing tragedy. It was awful. We then all spent an uncomfortable day at the beach together, running around and pretending to be upbeat – very false, but for a good cause, I guess.

It took about 6 more months before their dad left the house, but we kept talking. The boys went to the new house that he would be renting, which we dubbed the "Lil Blue House;" they saw their new room, new bunk-beds. He printed out our strange schedule every month (9 days with me, 5 days with him), and I have to say, the boys got it way before I did. I really stared at those months. I drew on them. I copied them, sent them to school (color-coded, natch!). It was a strange time. I was horribly depressed every time they left, but valiantly tried to say things like, "You're going to have a great time; I can't wait until you come back; have fun!" I even went to the doctor's office around this time at the urging of my dear mum and met with a physician's assistant regarding depression.

I will change the name to protect the innocent, but this doctor was one of those men that is SO good-looking that if he was walking down a city street, men and women would stop and stare, jaws dropping, angels singing. I've only met a few people who fit into this insane category, and my doctor for that day was definitely in this thoroughbred group. He looked like he had stepped out of a daytime soap opera, or from a hot firemen's calendar. So, in my head (I couldn't help it), I called him Dr. Hotty.

"What can I do for you today, Jeanne?" (I won't cry; I won't cry; I WON'T CRY.) "Well, I've been having a hard time since my divorce. Not specifically about the divorce, but more about when my kids leave for a few days; I think I have control issues and, and (sob, sob) I'm not sure where those days go." (Heaving sobs, losing all dignity). "Some days I feel like I'm engulfed by deep, still water."

Dr. Hotty thrust a tissue box in my face and looked like a deer caught in headlights. "I can prescribe some pills; they're not 'happy pills,' but I think they will help in a few weeks." My reply was "If they're not happy pills, why would I want them?" Smart ass.

I took these anti-depressants for about a year, and I guess they did help. I think – no, I absolutely know they numbed me out. My sweet neighbor of 15 years, Helen (89 years old) died at the end of that year, and my mom, who never cries, came over and sat on my porch and bawled. I didn't. I remember patting Mom's shoulder and thinking, "Why don't I feel anything?" I got off those suckers quickly. I'd rather feel than not feel and while I'm very, very grateful to Dr. Hotty for getting me through those initial days of feeling like I was engulfed in Jell-O and time had stopped, I wanted to feel again, the good, the bad and the ugly.

This took me a while, but I believe that the divorce was ultimately good for everyone. Out of a sense of respect, I won't go into details, but sometimes, the fairy tales don't come true and instead, you get what you need the most – independence and a greater sense of self. Kids are so resilient and the ex and I were committed to staying as positive as possible.

I would say it took a good year or even two years before our new schedule, our new lives felt "normal." Divorce can be an ugly, sad time, and I felt horrible to have put my kids through all of that business; they didn't have a "normal" family. I can only think of one other family on both sides of my family tree that went through a divorce, so I was definitely treading new territory. It is weird, however, how many, many acquaintances, teachers and even faraway friends fessed up to the demise of their marriage. That's what it ultimately felt like. Like my marriage had died, which is painful. However, as my dear mom always said (and I can hear her voice saying it as she has my whole life), "it all works out." And, it does.

ZACH'S MOTHER'S DAY POEM - MAY, 2004
(11 YEARS OLD)

"I love rhymes; I love to write a poem about New York and rhyme 'oysters' with 'The Cloisters.' And 'The lady from Knoxville who bought her brassieres by the boxful.' I just feel a sort of small triumph."

Garrison Keillor

Mom

My mom is not bossy,
From her, nice hugs,
To make me happy.
She doesn't do drugs.

About her hair, it curls,
It's black when I thought it was brown.
Beside her face, it swirls.
She's not a clown.

I like the word puzzles on my lunch bag.
They make me laugh and are always funny.
Don't worry, I won't nag.
Because I'm my mom's sonny.

Love,
Zach

READING, AND WRITING AND ARITHMETIC.....AND AIDS AND CONDOMS

ZACH HEARD A bit about AIDS in his 5th grade Health Class and...freaked out. At least, this is what was communicated to me in our traveling notebook from his classroom aide. So, at his bedtime, when it was quiet and calm, I asked him about it.

> **Me: "Did you learn about AIDS today in class?"**
>
> **Zach: (his eyes real wide and kind of "pretend" scared) "You can die from it, Mom."**
>
> **Me: "Okay, Zach-what were you told today?"**
>
> **Zach: "I don't know. It's about blood and YOU COULD DIE!"**
>
> **Me: "Wait, if you ever come across someone who is bleeding, try not to touch the blood. Here are the**

rules: Try to get help; try to wear gloves or have some kind of barrier, if you can. You can only get AIDS IF the person bleeding actually has AIDS and only IF it gets in your bloodstream (open cut), and all of this is RARE."

He liked the RARE part.

He liked that there were rules.

Then, I sort of ruined it by talking about my friend, Thom, who died from AIDS and what a terrible thing to happen to such nice people everywhere, and how it CAN be transmitted during sex; so, he should always wear a condom.

Me: "You know what a condom is, right? They talked about it in class?"

Zach: "Sure, of course."

Me: (thinking, THANK GOD…. but then just to make sure…I pushed it) "Great. So, just to make sure, what's a condom?"

Zach: (sighing) "It's where Grandma and Grandpa live."

Me: "Ummm….oh. Actually, that's a CONDO. Let me try to explain."

I think he heard the explanation, but maybe not. As the years have gone by, and more health classes have come and gone, Zach is *very* touchy whenever sex or sex education is brought up. I suppose we need to just keep talking about it or answer questions when they come up.

POEMS BY ZACH—AGE 11

FREEDOM

IF I WAS free to eat whatever I want, whenever I wanted, I would eat French fries for breakfast, lunch & dinner. Chicken Nuggets, McDonalds Chicken Nuggets, would be my snack. Dessert before breakfast, dessert before lunch, dessert before dinner, dessert before dessert. That is, I would have a whole bunch of desserts.

If I had the freedom to play whatever I wanted, I would play basketball, football, softball, bowling, street hockey and golf for ½ hour every day.

Upset

Well, you might not think this
But as you can see,
The only one upset here
Is me.

When I'm upset,
I start crying.
It's a terrible sight
When people are seeing me.

I feel like people don't want me around.
I heard of that on a CD-ROM.
Sometimes it makes my upset.
So, ummm, I gotta go.

WAAAAAAAAAAAAH!

RADIO BRAIN

"I'm never gonna stop music, it's like air to me."

Dr. Dre

"When I sing, people shut up."

Barbara Streisand

I HAVE THIS picture in my head of my son going off to recess after lunch in first grade. He's tiny and toddling alongside the building outside of the classroom doors and windows. He is actively talking to himself at a low volume and staring at himself in the reflections of the windows along his path. It was at this moment my brain conjured up the vision of a homeless man at a corner near our highway. This homeless man looked pretty well kept up, but always looked like he was having a conversation with an invisible friend. "Oh, that's what's happening (I think); that man is like Zach; he's talking to reassure himself or repeating bits of language he's heard before or from a movie or…."

My son teaches me every day. I won't say this aha moment was a great insight on my part, but I do look at that behavior differently now.

As a young adult, Zach has curbed that behavior in public, but it took a while. I'd say, "Hey, we all have conversations with ourselves, but we try to keep them in our heads; can you do that?" "Maybe…umm…can you whisper those out-loud things?" I'm not sure when it stopped, but he really doesn't do it much anymore.

What's strange is that when Zach was nineteen or twenty, he admitted that what he hears all the time in his head is music. Me: "All the time?" Zach: "Yep." Me: "Does it bother you?" Zach: "Only when it's from musicals or Barbara Streisand." (Oops, my bad.)

So, I tested him for a while. Me: "What do you hear now?" "Now?" It was always different and specific. Zach has a radio in his brain and he can't change the station or turn it off. I went on some websites and sure enough, other Aspergeans report this same symptom. Me: "Zach, we could probably go to the doctor and see if there's some medication that would either make that music stop or lessen it; do you want that?" Zach: "I'll let you know; I don't mind it." We've had several conversations regarding the music, but so far, he wants it with him….Babs and all.

LUCKY DUCKY

(Me and Zach driving to his weekly Drum lesson at the Seattle Drum School)

Me: "Look at that little dog walking with an orange sweater on!"
Zach: (In a mood) "Dogs get cold too."
Me: "I know; I always wonder about their little feet; they must be freezing; I've never seen little doggie booties before."
Zach: "You should get right on that, Mom."
Me: "Wanna go to Chipotle for lunch after your lesson?"
Zach: "Yes! (Remembering he is in a bad mood) "Except last time I went, whoever folded my burrito did a terrible job; they need to go back to "Burrito Folding 101" class."
Me: "It makes me think of napkin folding; I wonder if you could get a burrito folded like a duck? I WANT A DUCK BURRITO!!"
Zach: "ME TOO!!"

MUSIC

"Love yourself first and everything else falls into line."

Lucille Ball

Music has always been an intriguing part of Zach's life. Again, when he was in elementary school, he HATED attending the school choir during assemblies. I think all that noise just put him on sensory overload; I would joke and say it was because he had such a great ear for music, he couldn't stomach all those wrong notes (which are, of course, why school choirs can be so charming).

But I think it was more than the sound. Around this time, I was in a wonderful choir that put on really funny, charming shows and Zach didn't like that I was on stage. He didn't like it when his dad was on stage speaking either. Maybe the stage felt too much like a different world; I'm not sure. Zach really tried to conform; he would wear "painter's earphones," big, bulky earmuffs that would muffle the sound. He would still wince. If he saw anyone in the hallway wearing a choir t-shirt, he would grimace and make faces at them. I think it was painful for him and I wish that I hadn't made him sit there and struggle to get through it.

Early on, at age 7, I took him to his first piano lesson. I knew it was pretty early, but I just felt like learning music would be a piece of cake for him. In one respect, it was a Duncan Hines delight. He would look at his piano teacher's hands and copy them. Easy peasy. His teacher was a retired woman who taught for extra money; she was so patient. She had the kind of lamps where you touch the base three times and got three different strengths of lighting. Zach would wander around her living room and touch all of her lights. He loved those things; I can't imagine why I didn't get him one of those magical fixtures.

Zach, however, did *not* want to practice. I could see his mind go, "I can do this song; why do I need to overdo it?" Also, he didn't want to actually learn all the music notes. He didn't care two wits that the spaces on the musical lines spelled out F-A-C-E. Who cares? We went to piano lessons until he was ten, and he fought me every step of the way.

When he got to middle school, he had the opportunity to participate in a 2 week summer camp that his dad was in charge of through the Seattle Center. He took hip-hop dance and was surprisingly fantastic. He did a matrix move (slow motion, dipping backwards, avoiding all of the bullets) that impresses me to this day. So, of course, I enrolled him in this teacher's class thinking "This is it!" This is the musical thing he will excel at; I knew it was music; I just didn't know it was dance. Huh. What I failed to take into account was that the class was full of girls who were about 5 years younger, giggly and talkative. Zach didn't stand a chance. We went for a short time and then stopped; I could see the writing on the wall this time.

Then, Zach got "Rock Band" for his video gaming system and...wow. He was so good at drumming. His dad bought him some real drums and found a teacher at the Seattle Drum School. I still remember that first day. I walked right up to his teacher, Mike, a young man who seemed to be an accomplished drummer per his resume and his demeanor, and blurted out, "He's really good, just so you know. He's never really played *real* drums, but he just gets it; he gets the rhythms, the beats. You're going to be really surprised." Mike was polite, but he didn't say anything except, "Okay," and I could tell he was thinking I was a typical delusional mom with visions of grandeur. After the lesson, this man of few words came right up to me and blurted back, "Hey, he's really good! Anything I showed him, he could do right away."

I KNEW IT!! (Finally)

Doing drumming and finding what he absolutely excels at has been life-changing for Zach. He knows it's something that he can do better than most folks and can feel genuinely proud of it. Which is fan.tas.tic......something we all want in life.

PLAYDATES AND BIRTHDAYS AND GROUPS, OH, MY

"Worry often gives a small thing a big shadow."
Swedish Proverb

Q: "What did the birthday balloon say to the pin?"
A: "Hi, Buster."

Old Riddle

WHEN KIDS ENTER grade school, and in particular when you're a stay-at-home mom, there is this expectation that you will set up and have play dates. Ugg. It's like entering a dating pool. It really feels like you are "dating" these new parents so that your kid can get some social time. Now, if you like this new parent, all is good in the hood. However, there were several parents that I had to "break up" with and that was painful. One mother on our first phone call ever started vomiting out the most personal things about herself and her child in great, horrifying detail. Scary, weird stories. I made excuses for a while but then I had to be sort of brutal. "Zach is not ready for playdates; we can't get together because we're not ready; best of luck (it's not you, it's us)."

We did attend a ton of birthday parties during elementary school; I think Zach really enjoyed those days. There were always things done as a group (piñatas, crafts, games), very literal and clear. The rules were that you watched the birthday person open all of their gifts, sang the song and ate cake. He could get behind all of this business (except I do remember watching his face during the "song," sometimes he looked a little pained by it).

Zach's dad and I always tried to go great guns for our parties too; it was fun. I remember a royal theme where Zach's dad made an actual puppet theatre out of an old futon frame. It had velvet curtains. We bought some puppets and I wrote a show which we ended up taking to school a few times. I remember making an elaborate Halloween tunnel in our garage out of appliance boxes that everyone had to crawl through. It came complete with scary noises, squishy parts and creepy crawlies. I can't remember if Zach went through it or not; if I remember right, I believe he helped create it and did some of the effects for the party goers.

Throughout elementary school, we waited at a bus stop a few blocks from our house. That's where I met other "bus moms." Two lovely women in particular were so awesome; our kids seemed to really like each other and they would invite us over all the time. Sometimes just the moms would get together and have tea after the kids went along their merry ways and often, one of them would invite us over after school and everyone would run around outside or play in their rooms.

I have to say, I didn't really do my share of the inviting over. It didn't seem to matter, but I realize in retrospect, that I didn't really pull my weight. Granted, my house seemed just a little farther away than the other two houses, but it was more about me. I'm not sure why, but I always felt like the kids wouldn't like my house enough or that I hadn't "picked up" enough. Or maybe I'm a big weirdo and I felt uncomfortable. The other mothers *did* come over, just not as often as we went to their houses. This is where I confess some social anxiety myself and that I'm a bit of a recluse by nature. These bus moms and their families never made me feel like the dork that I truly am. They accepted me, Zach and Sam…and our lives were richer for it. Like most relationships in life, we all drifted apart. After my divorce, and the move to middle school and the bus moms getting jobs and girls and boys not "hanging out" as much, it was all different.

I really look back at that time with enormous fondness. Our kids were all so adorable and kind and there was a feeling of camaraderie that I miss. I will always be grateful for their friendships and wish loveliness for their families for all time.

THE GOOD HUMOR MAN

"Silly is you in a natural state, and serious is something you have to do until you can get silly again."

Mike Myers

EMAIL FROM ZACH IN HIGH SCHOOL—he sent it from one of his teacher's accounts as the teacher....

This is regarding something that Zach was worried about ever since the beginning of the school day. He's been worried about the fact that he thought his keys to his house fell out of his backpack in the middle of the street. He asks if you've ever saw them inside your house. If they have he'll feel very relieved. Naw, I'm just kidding, this is Zach who's writing this. If you saw my keys on the key rack, I'll feel relieved like the dickens. Thank you.

GOOD HUMOR, THE SEQUEL

(AGE 21) CONTACTS in his cell phone:

GRAMJAM (grandma)
LEEJEANS (me, Jeanne Lee)
JOHNNY (his dad who has NEVER been called Johnny by anyone, ever)
SIERRA MIST (a friend named Sierra)
PEG-A-LEG (a teacher named Peggy)
ALEXANDER TREBEK (an aide at school named Alexander)

IMAGINE

EVERY PERSON ON the spectrum is different. There are all kinds of checklists in the doctors' offices and Google-land, and there are hundreds of differences and things that are measured.

I think for Zach, his two biggest hurdles are sounds/noise and friendships/social cues. When he was young, I tried to put myself in his place, put on his high tops for a bit. I wrote:

> "I imagine sometimes what it might
> be like if I were autistic.

> I think when people talk I would sometimes hear the
> sound that all the adults in the Charlie Brown comics
> make. "Wah-wah-wah, wah-wah, wah-wah-waaaah."
> Too much talking. I would notice all the license plates
> on cars as they whooshed by me and I would try not
> to hear all the city sounds like noises that cars make,

people's voices, clicking sounds. I would love single
sounds like light rain while I'm lying on my bed or the
refrigerator noise in a quiet house.

School would be SO annoying; everyone listening
to one teacher drone on and on while chewing gum
noises, clicking pens, humming lights, dropping books,
opening and closing of binders, whisper, whisper.
On one hand I would love when a teacher decorated
their rooms so there was a ton to look at and on the
other hand, I'd hate it when there was too much chaos.
Everyone talks so much; it would be confusing to figure
out all of the hidden meanings behind the words. I
would wish everyone could choose their words more
carefully.

I would like it at work if I knew what was expected;
I would like it if I could accomplish task(s) and feel
successful as part of a team.

I would be thinking all the time and hearing music
in my head and getting confused when others didn't
understand or see or hear what I'm hearing. This would
be maddening. I would GET it, but that wouldn't make
it any easier.

I would want a friend I could share my thoughts with,
but I wouldn't know how to get one. How do you just
go up to someone and start something up? I don't
want to bother anyone or embarrass myself or get
rejected. I suppose it will get easier as I get older, but I

don't know. Maybe it's always hard to put yourself out there; everyone else makes it look easy, but I might be making that up. Maybe it's hard for everyone. Everyone probably has to put their fear away in a drawer and just take a chance. "

I'm sure I don't have a clue, but I think my acting background has helped me with Zach. I try to see the world from his lens as much as I can. While he has a hard time with empathy, I live in that place. Honestly, when I see those "lists" of things to look at when figuring out if someone is on the spectrum, I think I AM AUTISTIC. I'm not, but it wouldn't take much. One thing I've always been so grateful for is that Zach doesn't tend to withdraw from the world; he's always wanted to be around people and part of the action of life. This is good.

TODAY I AM A MAN

"I always wanted to be somebody, but now I realize I should have been more specific."

Lily Tomlin

WHEN ZACH WAS younger, around 4 or 5, we watched a Winnie-the-Pooh video, a VHS tape called "Stranger Danger." It wasn't the cute and endearing animated Winnie-the-Pooh; no, it was an adult in a very unconvincing costume. Actually, the word creepy comes to mind. Well, after viewing this travesty – I mean educational VHS tape – Zach considered anyone he didn't know to be nefarious and up to no good.

We'd go out to eat and he'd grimace and growl at everyone around us. I'd say, "Okay, so if you're with me or your dad, you're okay, no danger." He would then relax about it. We also came up with "code words." If someone came up to him and wanted him to get in a car, they would have to be able to say the code words. Although, we changed those suckers so much, I'm not even sure he would have gotten in a car with me.

Before he went to middle school, I asked him point blank. "If someone were to offer you a drink of alcohol or anything, a smoke of something or a pill, do you think you would take it?" Zach's reply was "Probably." This terrified me, so, I responded with (maybe not the best wording), "No, the answer is NO!"

Then, I said, "Ask me." So, Zach said, "Do you want to smoke with me?" I answered calmly, "No, no thanks….I'm good." I tried to explain that when he was 21 (legal), he could revisit whether he wanted to drink or smoke, but until then, it was pretty harmful to your body and brain. He started to moan, "I HATE the lung picture." I had forgotten about the lung picture. In one of his health classes at Einstein Middle School, they had put up a healthy lung vs. a lung where someone had smoked a lot of cigarettes for a long time. It was very disturbing to Zach. He actually would not go into the room until they moved it out of his sight line. (Even then, he wasn't happy it was up at all.)

I never know if all my harping and reminding and instructing means anything to my kids. Like anyone trying to reach their children, you hope you're saying the magic words that help your child make informed, good choices. If they don't, then hopefully, they can learn from their mistakes and carry on.

When Zach was a sophomore in high school, I got the following email from him.

Dear Mom,

Today when the school day started I had this very unpleasant experience. You probably wanna know what it is. Well, I'll tell you. Someone offered me drugs as in a cigarette. But right away I said, "I'm good." (as in "no") and then he was alright with it. He showed me he had them and I thought "Whoa, one of my friends is a smoker." I met him at the beginning of the semester. It's nobody you know by the way. When the period ended I thought and didn't say out loud, "Well, that was a very unpleasant experience." All I hope is that it won't ever happen again and if it does I'm just gonna try and be a man, dig down deep, and say something that sounds like "no." I feel very proud by saying I don't want to and I also feel really mature. I guess you can say now I am truly a man. Just thought you should know that.

From,
Zach "BaconWars"

(One, two, three….AWWWWWWWWWWWWW.)

"BACONWARS"

> "Do you want to know how good bacon is? To improve other food, they wrap it in bacon."
>
> **Jim Gaffigan**

So, IN HIGH school, Zach joined YOUTUBE. His moniker was/is "BaconWars." I really don't know why he created this particular name (I've never cooked bacon for him, <u>ever</u>); I think it's just a mash-up of Star Wars and bacon. Zach loves mashing two or more ideas or concepts together. For instance, he has loved the Nintendo character, Kirby for many years. So, he'll draw Kirby and layer on another character like Kirby as Wolverine or LeBron James.

He started creating videos for his page, his login. He created videos that showed his voice acting. Zach is a master of voice mimicry; my favorites are Homer Simpson ("I DON'T apologize; I'm sorry, that's just how I feel"), Stewie from Family Guy ("Cool *Whip*"), and many of the Looney Tunes characters. He really can imitate just about anything. I've always wanted to ask him to imitate me, but I am too terrified of seeing what that would look like. He would probably nail it. He also created some Ping-Pong trick videos, some videos from school and playing different levels of video games and so on. I think he has hundreds of them on there.

Zach loved that people would watch his creations. Here's an email from around the time he started his page.

Dear Mom,

I have a surprise for you. My most viewed movie is up to 1,012 views. Is that a big surprise or is that a big surprise? I hope you feel very happy for me. I feel very successful.

-Zach "BaconWars"

And people leaving nice comments? LOVED it.

Dear Mom,

My most viewed movie has 1,446 views and it has been favorited 13 times. There is one guy who seems to be really obsessed with it and this guy is kaitlynelynn. He/She posted three comments on the video and it's about the same subject "How He/She Likes It." I really don't know what to do. Should I block him/her or not? Please give me your thoughts on what I should do. Thank you.

-BaconWars

I was kind of worried that Zach might be someone who would share his address or phone number or meet up with someone from the Internet. So, I did sort of go overboard on the concept of privacy and not sharing or typing in our personal information. He listened!

However, a handful of people left negative comments and these comments would DESTROY Zach. I tried to stress that these people didn't know him; people are allowed to have their opinions; they needed to be more polite; just blow it off, please….but he would become despondent. Most of the time, if a negative comment happened, he would deem the creation unwatchable and take it off the Internet. He gave the "rudies" a lot of power.

Dear Mom,

You are not gonna believe this but someone posted a comment on Style Ping-Pong 2 saying "This is why you'll never get laid my friend." I did the right thing and blocked him. I mean, who is he to say that to me. But don't worry; I don't plan on that ever happening. But seriously though, the ones who post comments to me are putting me down all the god d*** time. Pardon my language, but OH MY GOOOOODDDDDD!!!!!!!!!!!!!! This is getting depressing. I don't wanna have this kind of thing happening ever again. I mean seriously, if one of those guys got ran over by a car and died I'd cheer. This is how mad I am. I want you to check that comment out and see for yourself why this is a stupid thing that's happening to me and a depressing thing. Thank you.

Zach, like all of us, wants to be accepted. He (to this day) seems heartbroken if someone calls him out or is mean; he considers that whoever it is to be "disrespecting" him and they are dead to him; there is no compromise or discussion; he seems incapable of understanding that when someone is mean, it has more to do with that person's problems than your own. It *is* hard to let go of negative comments (for everyone), but hopefully he'll learn how to navigate these roadblocks better as time goes by.

I, 100%, LOVE THIS KID

"Forty for you, sixty for me. And equal partners we will be."

Joan Rivers

ZACH USED TO want to buy a ton of music off iTunes. He would get gift cards for birthdays and Christmas and because I am a control freak, when he was in his teens, I would ask him to print out the lyrics and I would decide. (How do you spell control problem? JEANNE…)

The reason for this step was that Zach was/is a sponge. (Zachary SquarePants) I know all kids are to a degree, but Zach was an XXXXXX-large sponge and would imitate, move, sing, speak exactly like whatever he was interested in. This habit was fine if it was a socially acceptable thing like telling jokes. He went through a long period of liking wrestling. I think he liked the drama, the flair, and the theatrics. He would go to school and imitate the moves. That was not usually socially acceptable. He learned how to "beat box." That skill actually served him for quite some time; it was a socially accepted cool thing that he

would do for people. However, at some point, Zach wanted to
stop beat boxing and felt tremendous pressure from peers to
keep doing it and he was lost. He didn't know how to say "no
thanks;" I think because he didn't want to disappoint anyone
or it just felt uncomfortable. Either that or he could tell that
people (in high school) were only asking him to do it, in a way,
manipulatively, to make fun of him. I'm not sure.

I just didn't want Zach going to school and begin singing in
public about "Bitches and whores," or guns, killing, drugs, etc.,
etc. Master Imitator could do it and probably would do it. So,
I would stare at these rap lyrics and try to decide if even I knew
what the heck they were saying. I tried to give a LOT of leeway,
but he seemed okay during that time period to let me take a
look-see.

04/2008

I feel like you'll say "yes" when we look at Chevelle.

1. The Album I want it from is Clean.
2. You said it might 85% Yes and 15% no which is close to a yes.

E-mail from Zach

Zach no longer does this, but he used to talk in percentages
all the time. "I like Family Guy 90%;" "I want to go see
Anchorman 100%;" "I want to go to bed 40%." I loved how
he made it crystal clear how he was feeling through the
percentages.

OH, FALAPHEL

Zach and I in the car on the way home from drumming (teenage years):

Zach: I like to think up other words for swear words.
Me: Like when I say "Mother Hubbard" or "God…Bless America"?
Zach: Kind of.
Me: Give me an example.
Zach: Oh, fudgsicles! Oh, farmer's market! Oh, frozen berries!!
Me: I get it…Oh, Freaky Friday! Oh, Flintstones! Oh, fairy godmother!!

RAGE AGAINST THE MACHINE

"Let's get ready to RUMBLE!"
Michael Buffer, ring announcer for boxing and
professional wrestling

WHEN ZACH WAS around 5 or 6, I tried to join an "Autistic Parent Group." I went three times and vowed to never return. It was SO depressing. I guess I imagined it would be empowering, informative, or even, dare I say, inspiring.

No, sir-ee.

There were probably 40 people in desks, sitting in a big circle and vomiting out all this angst and worry. They kept harping on "teenage rages," teenage rages that were uncontrollable and horrifying. I (in complete naivety mode) thought, "Zach will never do this; I'm in the wrong place; I have no idea what these people are yakkin' about…this is nuts."

Ok, I can admit it now – I was wrong, wrong, wrong.

Probably for most of his high school years, Zach had rages. Something would set him off and he would get so, so angry, there was no reasoning with him. When he was calm, I told him that when it happened, I was going to direct him to his room. He might not want to go, but it was best for all involved. The rage would happen; I would tell him to go to his room, and he'd say "NO," but go.

The only thing I really learned over those years was that trying to talk to him, reason with him, deal with him during these nightmare times never, ever worked. I'd ask him later and he would describe "blacking out," not recalling how everything had escalated, why, or really anything much until it blew over. Many, many times these outbursts were fights between he and his little brother that ignited this ball of fury; they would often turn physical. It scared the crap out of me. I would ask his brother about it and try to read between the lines. I tried to suggest that Sam needed to be the one who walked away, but, honestly, sometimes Sam not only walked away, he ran away. He would lock himself in our bathroom or run next door to his grandma and grandpa's house. Just remembering some of these moments makes me feel completely ill.

Only once did I feel like Zach came close to hitting me; however, it only took that one time for me to reevaluate *everything*. I never ever thought he would hurt anyone, but I was wrong. Sure, he was "imitating" anger behavior he saw on the computer or television, and sure, the chances were slim that he would actually follow through on any of it, but....he could.

He had proven that he couldn't remember what had happened, what was said.

I would go into his room and just sit there with him; I wouldn't talk; I wouldn't even look him in the eye. At the very most, I would say "Just relax" or "Breathe" or "Stay calm." Sometimes I sat there for an hour. When his breathing seemed regular or when the room relaxed, I would start in low tones just talking to him calmly, like a white noise machine. "Zach, this hasn't happened for a while and it's important that you stay calm; we can figure this out."

I worried about my younger son, Sam, a lot. (I still do, actually. I have no idea how these few years shaped his personality and demeanor.) This behavior was in no shape or form, normal. He handled it most of the time with a ton of class, but it did shake him up. While Zach never hurt anyone, he was always substantially bigger than Sam, more intimidating. And a few times, they both got in some punches. I was told by friends and co-workers, "Well, boys will be boys", but that seemed like a pointless remark because those "sessions" left us all bruised and beaten up. It was not just boys being boys; it came out or nowhere, didn't make sense, and went from zero to a million incredibly fast.

I will say, reflecting on that "support group" I dismissed so readily, I wish I had paid more attention or stuck it out. (The folly of youth does exist.) I'm sure those families had some advice I could have heeded.

Here is an apology letter Zach gave to Sam – approximately 17 years of age.

"When you offend me, it's hard to find the words to explain so I get frustrated and angry. I hate having fights with a brother who's not autistic when I am because there's no possible way for me to defend myself with my words when I'm in the moment. I'm to blame for my own actions. I notice that the main time I ever do this is when you tell me to stop doing something. For me, it always feels like you're telling me to do something, when for you, it might feel as though you're asking. Also, whenever we argue, it feels as though I'm never given an opportunity to speak freely. Even though there are reasons for what happens, there's no excuse for violence and I get that it's unacceptable."

I think at the core of what was happening during this time was a combination of Zach comparing himself to Sam and not liking what he perceived as his own shortcomings, and also a complete lack of knowledge about how to have a healthy argument. Zach wanted to be rail thin like Sam, to have the social life Sam had, and I think it made him crazy that he didn't have those things. Also, Zach felt judged by Sam. Sam was often in a position of taking the lead and making decisions and he could get pretty bossy. None of this is a good excuse for what transpired. Honestly, Zach just wanted Sam to like him. I tried to make sure Sam knew that an honest compliment or a short, positive interaction with his brother would change his world. He tried. I could see Zach's whole being blossom when Sam was kind. I don't think Sam truly understood his power. He could bolster or deflate Zach in a single moment.

This was, in many ways, a good lesson for all of us. Thanking someone or being kind for even a moment can make or break someone's day.

Those rages are (mostly) gone. Oh, sure, there is an occasional blip, even an occasional bomb, but it's not the norm. I really don't know how or why – maybe age, maybe wisdom. I don't even feel like they're bubbling under the surface, ready to explode in a heartbeat. (Although if his sport team loses, watch out!) During those high school years, I would honestly feel like I better not leave the room and take a shower because in that time, the world could collapse. But eventually, Sam got busy with life, wasn't around as much, and when he was, we all seemed to get along pretty well.

I hope as they both get older, they will only get closer. I hope their bond and connection can stand the test of time. They're both very special beings.

WRESTLING

"There are a lot of similarities between dancing and wrestling. The costumes are the same, the spandex and all that, but you have to be light on your feet to do both, and you have to remember choreography."

Chris Jericho

AND SPEAKING OF wrestling, say what?

I'm not sure when Zach got a gander at the spectacle of wrestling, but wow, did it take hold. It started in high school, and of course, OF COURSE, he imitated what he saw. He would make grimacing faces, duplicate intimidating stances, made dramatic moves that made no sense to a casual passerby. He never did the wrestling moves on someone at school (I don't think), but his behavior was odd. I think all of us at that age are searching for our identity. Leave it to my kid to pick half-naked men in diaper pants, elaborate costumes and over-the-top dramatics to adopt.

I had to break it to him that it's all fake. However, it's like a crazy Las Vegas show. Because of my background in theatre and his exposure to attending a fair amount of performances, Zach got it pretty quickly. The wrestling thing though, the characters are so BIG, the show is so LOUD and all the moves are so pre-determined. He didn't care; he still loved it. It had good guys, bad guys, and pretty, scantily dressed girls.

I get it, but I hate it. I actually can't stand it. And, Zach tends to get obsessed and go way overboard. He would watch online, play games on his video systems, and imitate the moves. Ugg. However, both of my boys have made it clear they want no part of going to most theatre programs or listening to CDs of Broadway musicals. One note of Barbara Streisand and they both run for the hills. So, who am I to dictate what he spends his time on? He knows as a young man that he can't go around in life doing these moves. He hates that he gets obsessed and tries to cut back sometimes. He knows it's fake, but would prefer to enjoy it as if it's not. He's smart and making his choices.

I can respect those choices and still mourn the idolization of steroid induced, fake-tanned, really, really bad actors puttin' on a show that makes me cringe.

God, I feel old. YOU KIDS, TURN DOWN YOUR CRAZY MUSIC AND GET OFF MY LAWN!

SAM-I-AM

"A person's a person, no matter how small."

Dr. Seuss

WHEN SAM WAS about 7 or 8, I took him to a program in our area called "Sib-shops." This program, at Seattle Children's Hospital, came highly recommended for siblings who had brothers or sisters who were disabled. We only went a few times because Sam said he didn't want to go; I didn't listen and made him go to a few meetings, but I think they freaked him out. Honestly, most of the 2 hours spent in each session were the kids doing fun things like making tie dye shirts, swimming, and running around in active games, but at the beginning and end of the session, the leaders would have a circle discussion with the kids. Some kids talked about how they fed their siblings through their feeding tubes or how their brother or sister never talked, but they didn't care because they loved them. I think it was eye-opening for Sam and me. Living with someone with a ton of challenges can feel very isolating, as if you are the only family with issues, even though I knew intellectually that many, many families are not only going through our "stuff," but way, WAY more. Intellectually, I knew it, but it was easy to forget.

At the end of the sessions, some of the siblings would come in, and it was fascinating to watch the interactions. One small boy has stuck in my brain all these years. He was wearing a homemade vest which was COVERED with every kind of watch you could imagine, pocket watches, lady watches, man watches, kid watches; every color, shape and size of watch was sewn onto this vest and the young boy was calm and happy and staring at each one, one at a time. I'm guessing, but I imagine that he probably loved the numbers, colors, blinking, sounds. Fascinating.

Sam handled Zach's challenges so well when they were little; I think he truly loved him to the depth of his little kid heart. He would distract Zach, attempt to play games with him, laugh with him. I'm sure the turn-around was when Zach would flip out. Ahhh, puberty. I don't blame Sam in any way, shape or form. I tried to talk things through with him, even offered counseling, but Sam kind of withdrew from Zach. I think he was in mourning for what would be considered a "normal" brother relationship, a "normal" family life (no divorce).

He's always handled things pretty well, but all of this coupled with his puberty – well, during that time, he became very social with his friends, got a girlfriend and didn't really spend much time at home. I have faith that he has an excellent head on his shoulders, knows he is loved by many, and can come to me anytime to talk or help him figure things out (which he does occasionally). I do hope as he travels into adulthood he will see that Zach had to go through that hard period, but that he has come out the other end of the tunnel and is a smart, funny, awesome human being who could be a great friend/

brother as life goes on. (And, he could be awesome for Zach too; Zach idolizes Sam and wishes he could have a kazoodle of friends and a *girlfriend*.) Sam actually has made great strides in his interactions with Zach; I think as a young man, he finally sees Zach clearly. I even think, at times, Sam considers that HE knows better than ME what's going on with Zach which, at times, could be true. Maybe.

Sam became a natural leader at a very young age. He almost became the older brother, at one point. He learned compassion, patience and hopefully, he learned to give people chances because everyone has something to offer. I had to take Sam aside many times when he was younger and say, "Thank you so much for helping with Zach, but just to let you know, your job is to be a kid, have fun, certainly be respectful, but I'll make sure Zach's okay. That's my job. so, you can relax; it's out of your hands." *I'm sure* I made mistakes, but I tried my very best. I love both my boys immensely and consider them both stellar human beings.

INSIDE OF A BIRTHDAY CARD TO MOM

"Happy Birthday, Mom! I'm glad you exist."

Me too, buddy. Me too.

PUBERTY SUCKS

"Adolescence is just one big walking pimple."

Carol Burnett

HIGH SCHOOL WAS an interesting time. I take it back. It was kind of a hideous time.

During this time, I was trying to deal with finding a better job to take care of us financially, and when I got it, it was in downtown Seattle. I had a full-time job, farther away from home and didn't have the time to be as involved in school. I tried to justify it by thinking that it was time to let go; it was time to let Zach make some mistakes and learn, but I think Zach really needed more from me in the areas of friendships and social issues.

Instead, I focused on his homework. Honestly, what a waste. Zach's dad and I felt like *we* were going through high school. Finally, we cried "uncle." We fessed up to the teachers that we were spending hours and hours sitting next to Zach, painfully going over stuff, trying to have teaching moments, but doing a lot of the work ourselves. We opted for more pull-out classes (smaller) and more work experience. I had to resign myself to a high school certificate for Zach rather than a high school degree. This made me sad. Zach is so smart, but couldn't find it in his soul to care deeply about history – or most subjects, really. I always loved school and learning, but I recognize that most of it is not very literal or applicable without inferring a ton. Inferring stuff is not Zach's strong suit.

I think high school was pretty rough on Zach for other reasons too. I'm sure if you asked him about high school, he would say he liked the kids a lot. However, this was a time period when he became more aware of things in the social arena and it was incredibly frustrating. One example came from beat boxing. I believe there was a young man on American Idol at the time that beat boxed during his singing and Zach, being a master mimic, loved trying to imitate these rhythms and beats. He was pretty good and ended up doing some of it at school between classes or at lunch. After a while though, he became aware that some of the students were laughing and he couldn't figure out whether they were laughing *with* him or *at* him. He wanted to stop doing it, but he really didn't know how to casually say, "Not today," or "No thanks," or "I'm done with that business. He wanted to please people, but felt confused. He became aware that he might be doing something "wrong" socially and, well, that made him supremely unhappy. He didn't have anyone to ask, "Is this too much?" "Is this a joke?" He lashed out angrily and started making a big deal about it.

It was around this time that he said THE dreaded words to an assistant principal. "I'm just going to kill myself." Wow. When

I got this call, my first reaction was "He heard that somewhere; he doesn't mean it; he doesn't even know what that means." When I got to him, I asked him point blank, "Zach, do you really not want to be here, not live on Earth, and be gone?" Zach replied quickly, "No." I told him, "I'm not sure where you heard this, but it's very, very serious. If you say this to anyone, especially someone at school, they are going to think you're going to try to hurt yourself. They have rules. Anyone who says the **WORDS** you said, well, they consider that they are in trouble and need immediate help." He told me that he had heard it somewhere and that he didn't mean it, but he did say he was unhappy.

We got him to counseling. It helped. Here's what I think about therapists; I think there are some good ones out there; I think if you find the right person, it is a potentially wonderful relationship to have in your life. I also think that it's hard to find a good one. Zach's counselor was fine but I don't think her strategies really worked for Zach. He was with her for a few years and he made no leaps or bounds socially, but he had someone who listened. He knew that someone was trying to help him every week; a pretty young woman was going to take him seriously and make suggestions. I think the thing that really changed Zach's life during this time period was drumming. During this time, his dad recognized that Zach had an affinity for drumming on the video game, *Rock Band*. He found The Seattle Drum School and a fantastic teacher and it was a great fit. Taking drumming lessons and recognizing his natural talent did so much for his confidence. He knew he could do something that not many others could do. He was good.

Zach didn't like having an aide in high school, but she was so
patient and kind to him and us. There were other aides in the
pull-out classes for other students. One kid, whenever he got
upset over anything, would strip naked and scream bloody
murder. Yep, a naked teenager in the middle of the room would
go nuts. Zach's aide told me that Zach leaned over to this kid's
aide, patted her shoulder and said, "I feel your pain."

No wonder he hated school. He was trying so desperately to
fit in. He kept getting reminded through his aide, his pull-out
classes, and his inability to comprehend what was happening
socially, that he was struggling. I marvel that he kept going and
kept trying.

At one point, a really bad thing happened. From what I could
piece together, in the resource room which was a "hang-out"
place for kids at lunch or free periods, Zach was kidding
around with another boy. He was acting crazy like someone on
YouTube and at one point picked up a computer. The teacher
told him in no uncertain terms to put the computer down
immediately. I think in Zach's mind, he knew he wasn't going
to do anything to the computer; he knew he was just imitating
something he had seen; he knew this lady was ruining his
timing and fun and he lashed out. He lashed out – BIG time.
He verbally threatened this lady and her children. I couldn't
have been more shocked and disappointed. Of course, I knew
he was repeating something he'd heard; his assistant principal
and principal and special education teacher assured this woman
that Zach never had and never would hurt anyone, ever. But
here's the thing – this woman didn't know him. This tall,
formidable young man with a scruffy beard who was at the time

acting out and then threatening her and her family freaked her out. I completely understand. I was actually shocked that he was only suspended for three days. Well, he was banned from the "fun" room for the rest of his time there (about 2 and a half years), and banned from getting near this woman. This all seemed more than fair. It was bad….and wrong….and horrible.

In the meantime, Sam had joined his high school community. I don't think that went well. Sam seemed embarrassed and Zach became super jealous at the seeming ease with which Sam made friends and how well he was doing at school. What a tender age this is – trying to figure out the opposite sex, friendships, yourself. I didn't know how to help them both. I guess I kept hoping that Sam would chill out and Zach would have more successes.

I think that in life (for whatever reasons) some people "get it" and some people don't. What I mean is that some people understand that differences are exciting, interesting, and fantastic. These heroes take time, smile, investigate, connect and revel in the moment. They *know* that we are all special; we all struggle; we all should have a chance to shine. Some people don't get this notion; they really don't get it on any level. I don't blame them or think badly of them; I really don't. I just can't. I can only marvel at the missed opportunities for them. They don't get to share in a depth of living that eludes them. S'okay. I mean as long as they're respectful or are trying, it's okay with me.

It's the meanies that chap my ass. I have a hard time sticking up for me (I have a bit of the "doormat syndrome"), but watch out if it's my kids. I will fight – I will stand up anytime, anywhere, in order for my family to be protected from the ignorant, "I'm going to cut someone down to make myself feel better" vile bullies of the world. God, I hate bullies. I don't care what your past was—move past it; get over it and do it quickly. You do not get to torture someone else because you're miserable, at least not if I can help it.

Zach has been pretty lucky. Most of his aides "got it;" most of his teachers got it. He was mostly surrounded by very kind, loving, understanding people. Even the resource lady finally excused Zach and let him participate in some events that happened in her room (after he graduated).

Zach loved being surrounded by "normal" kids for those 4 years. Even though I wasn't able to help him develop a friendship there, he felt a kinship with those students. With few exceptions, he felt accepted and part of the group. The people at this school guided us to get Zach to participate in their "Transition Program" through the community college. This transition program would supposedly help give Zach some work experience and life skills classes. It did; it was just hard on Zach socially (once again). He yearned to be around kids who weren't struggling (outwardly or so obviously) so that he didn't have to face up to *his* challenges.

STUPID MAYANS

"I have a new philosophy. I'm only going to dread one day at a time."

Charles M. Schulz

So, SOMETIMES (IF you believe what you read) autistic people obsess about certain things. Okay, fine, it's true, but WE ALL DO. However, this was a hard one. Starting about 2010, Zach thought he was going to die in 2012. No, I take it back; he KNEW he was going to die. He would never have a girlfriend, see his twenties; the Mayans had predicted it; movies were backing it up (he only saw trailers on TV – never an actual movie) and it was going down.

We looked up reputable sites that debunked the theories. NASA wrote an open letter explaining point-by-point why it was all malarkey. Then, to my delight, at some point in 2012, someone discovered that the Mayan calendars went beyond 2012.

Yeah, none of that worked.

Zach tried. He did. I told him about Y2K, about other "religious" figures who proclaimed the end was near, how none of it never happened. He wanted to believe that everything would be okay; he wanted to believe that Hollywood took a seed of an idea and grew a "Children of the Corn" concept, but he just couldn't let it go. He was absolutely miserable and scared for at least 2 years. He made us all miserable (periodically) as well.

December 22 was a very good day.

When the next zealot or whatever comes to pass and states an end-of-the-world scenario, I've asked Zach to please, *please* remember that I will tell him the truth; I will try my best to always steer him in the right direction and not lie to him.

In the spirit of not lying, I did stay up all night December 21; I did. I mean, how could I not? Two years of trying to debunk something so obviously wrong does make one pause.

A few days after the date we shall never mention, Zach gave me a homemade card. It was on plain white paper folded in half. On the front was a very simple (and very accurate) picture of the world; on the "globe," the water was blue, the land masses were green. Inside, the card read as follows:

Dear Mom,

I now have three reasons to celebrate. Because you're awesome, Christmas is absolutely cool, and the Earth did not explode….meaning that we're still alive. I love that and you,

**Love,
Zach-y**

TRANSITION PROGRAM

"The road to success is always under construction."

Lily Tomlin

AFTER HIGH SCHOOL (or really in his junior and senior year of high school), we were introduced to the idea of our school district's "Transition Program." I was sold because the aim of the program seemed to be to give as much real job experience as possible and then some "living skills" like cooking, budgeting, health and other subjects that should probably be taught at every high school.

So, the job experience had its ups and downs. Zach's first job internship was with a store that made and sold marble tops and such for kitchens and bathrooms. Zach literally scrapped wax for months. Every day I'd ask, "What did you do today?" "Scrapped wax" was his reply every stinking time. He was so bored; I was bored for him. They seemed to really like him there and near the very end of his few months there, he finally got to pour wax into some molds (which was way more exciting than it should have been).

Next came a few months in a small café. This should have been a complete success because Zach would do some food prep, some cleaning, and get some experience with a cash register and customers. Nope. It was a dismal failure for two reasons. Number one was that the woman who owned the café was a stone cold bitch. One day, she looked at him and said, "You're taking 5 extra minutes on your break; so, I'm going to have to let you go." Zach left that day for the bus and broke down sobbing; he'd been fired and he really had no idea why.

I frantically called and emailed the school and came to find out he wasn't fired; the woman was *kidding*. It was some sort of perverse joke. What the hell?? She said she was joking and had just wanted Zach to watch his break time. Well, Zach is a master of time watching. Even in his preteen years, if I said "You have one hour on the computer," he would watch the clock and in one hour (exactly) get off the thing. So, I *knew* Zach was watching his time. A few weeks later, this same woman told Zach he wasn't washing the dishes fast enough and to not come back. He came home very confused. "I might be fired again; I'm not sure."

This time, the email came back – this time Zach was actually fired. The reason was mostly because of his behavior with this woman's DOG which was the second reason this café sucked. Almost every day when Zach went to work, there was a small wiener dog roaming around the kitchen and restaurant. Zach is terrified of dogs, any dog. Granted, his fear is over-the-top (the dog was very old and graying on his muzzle and very, very slow moving), and we tried to work with it, but here's my question: *why was there a dog in the kitchen and restaurant?* Isn't that a health code violation?

I looked up on Yelp and other review sites and this lady treated her customers horribly, telling patrons she ran out of coffee (in a *coffee* shop), laughing at them and on and on. So, I contacted the health department. Yes, I did. I reported her and her damn dog.

The health guy said he contacted the lady and she told him it was her "roommate's" dog and it was *not* in the kitchen and that it hardly ever came to work. LIAR. Anyway, I told him that the dog was there all the time and the only way to prove it would be to actually go there. He said they rarely go "onsite," but that he would check back in with her at a later date. I don't know if I made any difference at all; I just know that within a year, the café was closed and has never reopened. It might have been me (God, I hope so) or simply that she was a complete nightmare and it caught up with her.

His next job was awesome. Finally. Thank goodness. Zach interned at a local grocery store. They liked him so much that they started putting him on their schedule between two departments (which I guess was highly unusual), the Bulk Department and the Pizzeria. In the Bulk Department, Zach would fill up bins, churn the peanut butter, create displays and in the Pizzeria, he would fold pizza boxes and create some of the pizzas. On his last day there, he helped customers and I went and watched from afar. He looked so happy, listening to orders, scooping them up and handing them to the patrons. I wish he could have done that part for much longer; he seemed to really enjoy it.

The job following the pizzeria was at a small movie theatre and it was fantastic. He cleaned, stocked the candy, made the popcorn, sold concessions (he knew all the prices immediately) and took tickets and money at the door. The other employees were all around Zach's age and were really nice to him. I think he liked it there even more than the grocery store. I think he could have even worked there eventually, but we could never figure out transportation. The city buses didn't really go to where the theater was and the hours would have been late on the weekends.

The hardest part of the Transition Program for Zach was being around other kids during class time. He is very high functioning and eventually he seemed pretty bummed that he was with these students because, I think in his mind, he didn't belong with them. He would say "they are not my people." I don't think he meant to be cruel at all; I think he just started feeling badly about himself. He missed being around the other high school kids and would actually act up in class often. I would get emails and phone calls regarding Zach saying something rude or slamming his way out the door. He'd get frustrated at how slow the classes were going and say "it's disrespectful." In his defense, at least according to him, he felt like they were repeating the classes every year; in the teacher's defense, I'm sure she was modifying and adding things and Zach didn't pay attention enough to realize this was happening.

I wish Zach could have a deeper sense of how special these kids were; that everyone deserves respect and admiration for their skills and talents no matter what. It seemed like the kids who admired Zach the most, bugged him the most.

I have worried from time to time about Zach's mental health. Because he doesn't have a friend to hang out with or talk to, he spends a great deal of time with himself and technology. He thinks up projects for himself (lists, drawings, YouTube videos, editing projects) and most of the time seems content. Every once in a while, he gets sad. "I'll never have a girlfriend—ever!" or "I have no one to hang out with!" I'm someone who tends to keep to herself; I'm not super social. What with working full-time and raising the boys, I never had a lot of extra time. I wonder if I had made his social life a priority, would I have set a better example? Or if I had poured more energy into this when he was younger, would he have been around other kids more often. I don't know. We're all super in some areas and deficient in others and I hope Zach understands that as life goes on, I will always try to help him. Maybe his work experience, drumming, a hobby or an internship will lend itself to helping Zach forge some friendships. It's important.

GRADUATION SPEECH
JUNE 2014 (21 YEARS OLD)
(THEY GAVE THE BOY A MIC!)

This is finally the year
That I go and graduate
The SCC (Shoreline Community College) college
In Washington state

I'd like to thank the Academy
Nah, I'm just playin'
But I will comment on the praise
That y'all be displayin'

That mother and father of mine
Are whom I'd like to thank
If this was a video game
They'd get an A rank

And now, let me give you
A word that you should follow

And I'm not talking about
A bitter pill to swallow

Never let jerks
Tell you how to feel
You're the only one that
Can tell yourself what is real

Alexander (an assistant in his program),
you are <u>not</u> an X
You are a **check**
And in my book
You'll always be "Trebek"

I've had many different times
Neutral, bad and good
And it's always felt nice
When I act like I'm from the hood

And after 3 long years
The burden of school is off
It's now time for me
To celebrate,
Mazel tov.

I SECOND THAT EMOTION

ZACH (AGE 21): (Staring at his Grandma's old Toyota sitting in our driveway, then shaking his head; she was "gifting" Sam and there it sat....)

Me: What's up, Zach?

Zach: I don't want to be jealous; I want to be happy for the guy. I think I'm just going to not think about it.

Me: Good plan. Jealousy is one of those emotions that doesn't help anybody.

Zach: Well, I don't like it.

SOCIAL SCENARIOS

"When God sneezed, I didn't know what to say."

Henny Youngman

SOMEDAY, ZACH WILL have independence. I can imagine him with a full-time job somewhere around a nice group of people. He feels good about what he's doing and is successful. I can also picture him taking care of himself in his own apartment; I sort of see a roommate too.

That place totally works in my head. Where I get concerned are the "glitches" that happen every day for every single person on planet Earth. When something doesn't match the normal script, the normal way that Zach pictures it, he either freezes or gets totally frustrated.

So, at age 21, I'm starting something I should have started a long time ago. Actually, his dad and I talked about it, and every once in a while, we are both going to present a particular scenario for Zach to consider. Then, we can offer some suggestions or insights.

Some I've tried so far:

1. You're waiting at a bus stop and a homeless man or woman asks you for money. What would you do or say?

   We actually went over appropriate responses like "Sorry, I don't have any cash," or just handing someone a few dollars if you want or just walking away.

   Then, of course, it happened and Zach was *so* frustrated. "I gave the guy a dollar and then he was in my face and wouldn't stop talking to me." I asked, "What was he saying?" Zach responded angrily, "I have no idea."

   We decided, next time "No Cash" and maybe he could contribute to a charity for the homeless like the Salvation Army would be an easier way to help out.

2. You're in your apartment alone; there's a knock on the door. A really pretty girl your age is standing there; she tells you that someone stole her purse and she needs to use your phone. What do you do?

   "I give her my phone."

   Great. Sooooo, Zach is very trusting (especially with young women). So, I explained that even though she was a pretty, young girl, she was a *stranger* and it was appropriate to be at least a little bit on guard. If you really want to hand a stranger your phone, step outside, lock your door, and hand her your phone. You could also say "No," or "Try a store down the street."

3. You're at work and someone you've worked with for a few months starts telling you their troubles; they are about to be evicted from their apartment and they ask if they could live with you for a while (maybe on your couch). You technically know this guy, but you don't really know him very well. How would you handle it?

The response was, "I don't know" which is fair. We went over some ways to deal with it and some scenarios that could happen.

DDA, SSI, LMAO

"Why do they call it rush hour when nothing moves?"
Robin Williams

So, THERE'S HELP out there. However, there are many, many hoops, rings, buzzers and levels of Dante's inferno to traverse in order to get that help. Perhaps that's how they screen out the wannabes. I'm kidding. No one in their right minds wants this kind of help. It's just hard any way you look at it.

When Zach was formally diagnosed, it was suggested that we "put our names" on a list at DDA (the Developmental Disabilities Administration). We were on that special list for about 13 years. This program supposedly helped families afford respite care, counseling or other helpful services. When Zach was sixteen, we got the call. Yes! Better late than never!

Whoa. Don't saddle up quite yet cowboy.

No, services weren't forthcoming. First they had a telephone interview. Then, they came out to my house for an interview.

Not intimidating at all. In the initial interview, this very nice young woman asked me a kabillion questions about Zach, personal hygiene (teenage years, Axe, natch), school, home life and other aspects of life. Then, she wanted to interview Zach.

Now, I will admit to considering prepping my son, but I honestly didn't know what that would entail. Do I hope he flies high and presents himself so well that we don't qualify? Do I ask him to tell this lady every YouTube video he's ever seen in hopes of presenting a true, but potentially eye-opening experience?

In the end, I did nothing except to say to Zach that a person was coming to interview **US**, that if she asked any questions, he should listen, be himself, and try to answer her. I do remember one question. She asked, "Zach, if you looked out the window, and you saw your neighbor's house on fire, what would you do?" He thought for a minute, threw his hands up in the air and started yelling "Fire! Fire! Fire!" and running in tiny circles. Now, there's actually nothing wrong with that answer; he would, in fact, be alerting everyone in the area to what was happening. However, when she pressed further (obviously wanting him to talk about calling 911 and/or actually telling someone), he didn't come up with that answer.

He then started imitating heavy metal music hand signals with appropriate head banging.

We were accepted.

The truth is that most of the time, Zach acts like whatever "normal" is. Truly. He laughs, tells jokes, spends too much time on the computer, and listens to his music. However, when problems come up, as they inevitably do on a daily basis, he can get very stuck. Whatever is happening is NOT matching up to the picture in his head, and it's baffling. And frustrating. And infuriating. Something that isn't supposed to be happening is happening and damned if he knows how to deal with it.

Then, it was *strongly* suggested that we start trying to get Zach on SSI (Social Security). I was again conflicted. I believe in Zach; I believe in having high expectations. So, thinking that Zach will never hold more than a part-time job and probably a low-paying one makes me crazy-pants. This smart, funny, capable young man has a place in this world. Good Lord! If some of the people I've seen in the world have jobs, Zach can. Well, after a few bad internships (work experiences through school), I acquiesced. Plus, people at school who have dealt with the systems and with kids similar to Zach convinced me that this was a hurdle worth jumping over, because if he was accepted, other things would follow. Things like having a "job coach" for his whole life who could help him navigate through any conflicts at work or give him training would become available.

Fine.

Oh, there are forms to fill out? Got it. Oh, you need records from EVERYBODY EVER? Done. Oh, another interview? Fine, fine, fine. His grandmother took him in and it was a 2-hour interview with a psychologist. Well, Zach didn't pass or did pass (depending on how you look at it). We were denied. "No worries; everyone gets denied the first **few** times; just keep reapplying; it's possible at some point, you might have to get a lawyer." What? No way. I'll apply again if I have to do it, but no freakin' lawyers. I still think it's all sort of stupid; Zach doesn't need this service. Wait, he might. What do I know? Plus, I hate failing a test.

So, I redid all the paperwork and this time his dad took him in for his interview. He reported that it took about 20 minutes and Zach got accepted. What the – what? Never underestimate sending a guy in to do the job; it's horrible, but unfortunately it can make a difference. John used to purposefully come to all of Zach's IEP meetings at school in a white shirt and tie, carrying a briefcase and pulling out a legal pad and a pen and documenting things said during the meetings. I could tell that everyone took notice. It's sad, but a reality of this world. I know that when I purposefully exude all the confidence I can muster, dress nice, put on some make-up, actually brush my hair, I can own the room. I just don't do it that often.

So, now Zach gets SSI money. Easy Peasy. NOT.

I feel like this service is a part-time job for me. First of all, I'm confused about what we can use the money for. I know clothes and things for Zach like his drumming lessons, and classes are okay and I know I need receipts for everything which I keep in a month-to-month binder. I know that he can't go over $2,000 or everything grinds to a halt. Also, the first time he got a part time job for about 2 months. For the love. All the phone calls needed were extraordinary; they had to know when, how many hours, the location, the manager's name, wage, we had to send the pay stubs every 2 weeks, call this number, send this form.

And, and, every time any action is called for, there's a literal threat that if you make a mistake, give the wrong information, hit the wrong button, you are legally responsible and can be jailed. That's too much pressure. I can't even handle it when a police car is in back of me on the highway; I'm SURE I'm going to be pulled over....even though I'm not doing anything wrong, EVER.

Ugh.

Zach is also plugged into a government agency that will, perhaps, maybe help him find a job. Here's my experience. His first helper, a very nice young woman who got pregnant and was only with Zach for about 6 months, accomplished nothing. She did try though. She got him some interviews that were fairly close to our house; she found places where she had some relationships; she didn't however, listen well to what we wanted for Zach. I had the feeling that in order for her to do well in her job, she had to check some boxes every month on a list. The "list" was important, and honestly, I guess I understand it. But, in order to check the things on her list, she seemed to frantically take him on things that didn't make sense. She took him to interviews that told her they'd be hiring later; so, she should check back. Why is he interviewing for things that don't exist?

However, the next dude who took over for her did NOTHING, NOTHING, NOTHING (echo chamber). Well, he did meet with us once. He did send a lot of emails. After, about 6 months, he took Zach to an interview at a burger joint. Hey, Zach is an incredibly capable young man and I can't freaking

believe the wading through mud that happens; it drives me
insane. I took a day off work, took Zach's references and
résumé to Costco, introduced myself to a manager and had
a short meeting with her explaining that while Zach did an
online application, I wanted a few minutes to explain to her
what a fantastic, loyal, hard-working employee he would be
and explain quickly his background. I ran home, emailed the
dude, who wrote back, "Would you like me to follow up with
Costco?" YES, YES, YES I WOULD. Okay, I'm sure these
people have way too many people they're helping; I know; I do;
I swear....but for pity's sake.

Now, I've been informed that Zach is eligible for a "waiver."

What the f@ck. I mean...what the falafel.

I AM NOT A DOORMAT
(OR I AM NOT A PIRATE, PART DEUX)

So, Zach has had some troubles in his young adulthood with aggressive sales people. Once, during a PAX convention (Penny Arcade Expo/popular gaming festival) at age 21, while he was waiting for his dad to pick him up, some "musicians" approached Zach. They showed him their CDS and wanted to give him one. Zach's a musician; so, he thought, "Why not?" THEN, these scammers told Zach that they were accepting donations. He gave them $10 bucks. At this point, something went awry because they must have seen that he had more money. He swears they didn't accost him or hold him up, but whatever the exchange happened to entail, Zach walked away with all of his money gone – $80 bucks.

I've wondered if they did accost him and he's too embarrassed to say anything, but it could be they just gave him a sob story; I don't really know. He was so upset. He didn't want to give them all of his money, but he didn't know the right words or what was the right thing to do. We came up with some strategies; we practiced saying "NO," walking away, leave the area, no eye contact; we talked about it; we practiced it. He uses his debit card more often and doesn't carry too much real cash in his wallet. He knows there are scammers in the world and he needs to guard against them.

Cut to 2 years later and he took a bus to a local mall in search of a Christmas gift for his dad. In our malls, especially during the holidays, there are a million kiosks set up in the middle of the walkways selling all sorts of things. They're usually pretty aggressive. *I* never make eye contact with those people, and often hug the sides of the walkway in hopes of avoiding them. Well, a young woman at a perfume/cologne kiosk saw Zach and went in for the kill. "Do you want to get some cologne for your dad?" Zach says he said "No." "Well, I can give you 7% off today, but don't tell anyone!" Zach said he got confused; again, he wasn't sure what to say or do. In my mind, this seemed like a repeat of the PAX situation, but often different locales don't really translate.

I actually called the kiosk and said to this young woman, "Hey, I know that you're trying to sell your perfume and Zach needs to take this situation and learn from it, but in the future, could you be more sensitive? My son is disabled and he didn't want your cologne. He said no and got further pressure from you; he was confused and upset. This woman cut me off and screamed "NO REFUNDS!" At this point I said, "Look, I never mentioned a refund; I'm trying to share some information with you and just want your reassurance to try to be more sensitive. She roared, "I HAVE CUSTOMERS; I CAN'T TALK TO YOU!" Then, I got mad. "Give me the name of your manager, his or her phone number and your name. She spat it out (reluctantly) and then hung up.

Well. Okay, then. I contacted the mall, found the proper channels and wrote a detailed email with names and numbers and what I wanted. Then, I spoke to Zach's dad because he can be very intimidating; I told him the whole story and he seemed onboard to go to the mall and speak with someone. Zach's brother wanted to go too, but I discouraged it (even though I was super pleased that his reaction was one of protection).

I then recalled a few years ago when a young woman at Marshall's accosted **me** about getting a credit card. "No, I don't need a card." She pushed; I said no; she kept going; I said no; she frantically spewed out details; I relented. I relented! Damn it. I didn't want that card. I never used it, but I let her win. Maybe it's genetic.

I really talked to Zach's dad for a few reasons, but mostly it felt like a parenting call to arms. We were told when Zach was a teenager to go to court and get guardianship. I didn't want to do it. I didn't fight super hard or anything, but the thought of stepping into court, in front of Zach and saying that we needed to make his financial and medical decisions because he wasn't capable felt wrong. I just honestly didn't think he would need it; he's very high functioning and very compliant with me. However, it's becoming clear that in a world of potentially super aggressive sellers, people or even friends that Zach has a hard time saying no. I understand it. I do. I've struggled with not wanting to be a doormat for years.

So, I told Zach that we were going to look into guardianship, explained what that meant and asked what he thought about it. He took a moment, looked at me and said, "Does this mean

I'm more disabled than I think I am?" OH MY GAWD. My heart dropped because I don't want him to think that or plant that seed. So, I told him the truth. "Don't think of it that way; think of it more like a good way for your dad and I to be able to help if you get in a jam. If a scammer gets the better of you, we would have a legal way to help you get out of a bad situation. We would be your safety net." He seemed genuinely okay with that answer.

I'm not sure what the future holds, but it's a little shameful that there are people who prey on the innocent, who can scan a crowd and zero in on the one person that they could take advantage of big time. Yes, Zach had a part in this dance, but I guess I just wish the world could be different. I wish for compassion and kindness and no one who wants to scrape their boots on me or my kid.

BACK TO THE FUTURE

"Great Scott!"

Dr. Emmett Brown

I DON'T KNOW what Zach's future holds; I know what I hope. I hope he gets into a band full of cool, interesting human beings and they totally rock it out. I hope he finds a job that he can feel good about, working with nice people and feel proud of his successes. I hope he can have the apartment that he's talked about having, hopefully with a nice roommate. I hope someday he meets a wonderful girl who will love him because he's pretty damn awesome.

I've learned so much about communication from Zach. I am a champion of quiet, indirect talks because that's what works the best. We talk often in the car about important things that have happened during the day. We are both looking forward and we are both engaged. Zach will often turn off the radio and close the windows; I know when that happens, we're talking. I really enjoy talking to Zach at night when there are no noises or at least not as many that I can hear. The day has wound down, the world has calmed down and it's the perfect time to chat. I will often get fascinating texts and emails from him.

In 2006 when he was 14 years old, Zach sent me an email that ended with "I'm in your fan club, Mom." I've treasured that comment for years; I don't care if he got it off of a movie or a YouTube video; he wrote it to me. This book, in small measure, was fueled by my being in Zach's Fan Club....not just because he's my kid, but because he is kind, funny, smart and a gentleman. I believe in you, Zach.

Rock On.

**"The easiest thing to be in the world is you.
The most difficult thing to be is what other people
want you to be.
Don't let them put you in that position."**

Leo Buscaglia

"May the Force be with you."
Qui-Gon Jinn